Forest Under My Fingernails

Forest Under My Fingernails

Reflections and Encounters on the Long Trail

WALT MCLAUGHLIN

HERON DANCE
PRESS

HᗕRΘN DΛNCᗕ PRᗕ᙭᙭
179 Rotax Road
N. Ferrisburg, VT 05473
www.herondance.org

Watercolors by Roderick MacIver
Designed by Ann O'Shaughnessy

Maps by: Map Adventures
Portland, Maine

For information about special discounts for bulk purchases,
please contact Ingram Publisher Services at 1-800-961-7698.

This book printed on Rolland Cascade New Life recycled paper
and printed in the United States.

ISBN: 1-933937-04-1

In memory of Roland Boucher

ACKNOWLEDGMENTS

I want to thank Steve Bushey for making the map in this book, Walt Franklin for critiquing the manuscript when it was still rough, and Jerry Siegrest-Jones for providing me with enough old lumber to build the three wooden food containers used during the trip. Thanks also to my brother, Greg, as well as Bruno, Anne and Sonny, Husky, Mr. Clean, Wena and the many other hikers who helped me along the way.

As always, I am indebted to my wife, Judy Ashley, who helped make both the trip and this book possible. A special thanks goes to her for encouraging me in all my endeavors, no matter how offbeat or impractical they might be.

One

THE MANIC CRY of a distant ovenbird breaks the late morning silence as I struggle breathlessly up the steep Pine Cobble Trail with a fifty-pound pack tugging at my shoulders. Even though it's only the first day of June, summer already has a firm grip on these mountains. The refreshing coolness of early spring is a blurred memory. I sweat, gulp down water, then sweat some more despite the deliberately slow pace I keep. My foot barely misses a garter snake. The intoxicating smell of unseen wildflowers wafts through the air. Chipmunks chatter from the crackling leaf litter on forest floor. My walking stick clicks against dusty rocks strewn haphazardly across the beaten path. After several months of preparation, planning and waiting, I am finally on the move. That white-blazed trail stretching the entire length of Vermont begins just ahead.

The surrounding forest looks familiar but I'm not quite in sync with it yet. A part of me is still in a Williamstown cafe, enjoying brunch with my wife, Judy, while listening to classical music. It will take a while to match the natural rhythm of things. Several thresholds must be crossed before that can happen. The first will come in a matter of hours; another after a night in the woods; yet another in a few days. I relish this gradual return to a simpler existence, yet something deep inside me recoils in mute terror from it. More has been abandoned at the trailhead than the mere amenities of modern living. With a little coaxing from the forest, a wilder self will slowly emerge but only at the expense of something more refined, genteel. It's a trade-off to be sure.

Mt. Greylock looms in the thick haze to the south while I take a short break on a rocky outcrop called Pine Cobble. A towhee sings, then a hermit thrush. A pair of dayhikers lounge among jumbled rocks a few yards away. The town of North Adams sprawls in the valley below. The air is strangely still. After catching my breath, I wipe my brow with a sweat-soaked bandana then turn northward. A few minutes later I'm on the Appalachian Trail, rapidly approaching the state line as shafts of afternoon sunlight punch through the thin canopy overhead.

The Long Trail starts in the middle of nowhere, on the other side of a small wooden sign marking the Vermont-Massachusetts border. With three and a half miles behind me already, this beginning seems somewhat out of sequence. I sign into the trail register anyway, indicating my final destination as well as the estimated length of my stay in these woods: Canadian border, thirty-three days. The afternoon quiet is punctuated by the high-pitched whine of mosquitoes, black flies and other airborne insects. The commencement of such a grand journey couldn't be any more understated. Squirrels and chipmunks chatter nervously, then fall silent. So much for fanfare.

I plant my walking stick then take a step. For the next hundred miles, the Appalachian Trail and the Long Trail will be one in the same. Just beyond Sherburne Pass, the trail splits. At that point, the AT veers east towards New Hampshire while the LT continues north another one hundred and sixty-seven miles to Canada. I have a long walk ahead of me.

My plan is a simple one. I will venture as far north along this trail as my rather non-athletic body will go. It would be nice to hike all the way to Canada but I don't expect to make it that far. With troublesome knees and nearly twenty pounds of excess fat hanging from my middle-aged frame, I'll be lucky to make it half that distance. That would be okay. Can always finish the trail some other year. The main thing is to spend as much time as possible in these woods. Running wild is what this trip is all about. The trail is merely the vehicle. Sixteen days is the longest I've ever been in the woods without interruption. I'd like stay out here longer this time around. If necessary, I'm willing to take up temporary residence at some alpine pond in order to attain that goal. But even that might be out of the question. It'll come down to whatever the knees dictate.

Pink lady's slippers bloom in small patches here and there along the trail. Yellow clintonia, trout lily and other spring wildflowers are even more abundant. But starflower rules the day— its tiny, white petals shining brightly along the trail like a grounded constellation. Wildflowers are reason enough to brave the swarms of bloodsucking little beasties that thicken the air this time of year. Towards the end of summer, the trail will be crowded with happy hikers enjoying bug-free walks. I prefer late spring and early summer, gladly exchanging a little blood for a few snorts of pollen and the deep solitude that accompanies the bloom.

A barred owl startles me with an unexpected call. I, in turn, surprise a wild turkey wandering lazily up the trail. A jet roars overhead, temporarily forcing the seemingly infinite green world around me into perspective. I resent the intrusion but forest silence returns quickly enough, thus assuring me of the resiliency of nature. It's no small consolation.

I make good time traveling over easy ground. I roll into Seth Warner Shelter with plenty of daylight to spare. Drawing water from the stream nearest the shelter, I make the acquaintance of a frog sitting motionless upon a rock. A raven croaks in the distance, reminding me of wilder country much farther north.

Something pulls me that direction but right now I'm happy enough to be in the Green Mountains—my home turf. The young, fresh leaves in the treetops overhead flutter in a gentle gust of wind. The air is rife with the earth's rawest smells, reminding me of sacred, secret places. This trip is off to a good start.

At dusk, a twenty-ish fellow charges into camp. He drops his pack on the picnic table in front of the shelter. He is accompanied by a white dog who sniffs intently around the shelter. I tend a few burning sticks in the fire pit while the newcomer unpacks. Like most long-distance hikers, he goes by a trail name while he is out here. He calls himself Puff. The name has something to do with a Grateful Dead song but I miss the connection. Shed is the dog's name. By the way Shed roams about the edge of camp, it's apparent that he feels right at home in these woods. Evidently, Puff has taken him hiking before.

Like me, Puff is headed for Canada. His plan is more ambitious than mine, though. I hope to average nine or ten miles a day. Puff wants to do twelve to fifteen. He intends to hike the entire Long Trail in three weeks—not counting a few days off-trail towards the middle of the month to attend a couple of rock concerts. In order to achieve that goal, Puff has committed a detailed itinerary to paper. I, on the other hand, have a telescoping fishing rod and a pair of binoculars which I intend to put to good use. To each his own.

As the campfire diminishes to glowing embers, we bed down for the night. I slip beneath a large rectangular piece of netting called a mosquito bar. The black flies disappeared a couple hours ago but mosquitoes are still buzzing about the netting. Puff burrows deep into his sleeping bag to avoid the menace. Shed paces back and forth before settling down with a heavy sigh. The night is full of creatures just beginning to stir but Shed doesn't bark. For that I am grateful. A good night's sleep is needed. Big day tomorrow.

Two

"IN THE TRADITION of other early New England trails," my guide book says, "the Long Trail is steep, boggy and rugged." As I slowly ascend a 3,000-foot unnamed summit, this simple fact is brought home by my own heavy breathing. The path underfoot is unimproved to say the least. Mud quickly covers my boots. The overgrown trail shoots straight up the mountain. The white rectangular blazes painted on trees are the only assurance that I haven't lost my way. This isn't the Long Trail as I've known it. Farther north and closer to home, there are wide, deeply rutted paths up all of the major mountains. But the urban herds don't hike this southernmost portion of the LT. Here only a couple sets of relatively fresh boot prints have been pressed into the soil. Very few waterbars stretch across the trail and there is even less stonework. Not that I'm complaining. In a way, the trail's roughness suits my mood as well as the surrounding wild landscape. Besides, it is always a pleasure to walk where few have walked before.

Atop the unnamed summit, I review my maps along with a description in *Guide Book of the Long Trail,* committing to memory the lay of the land immediately ahead. Just before leaving

Seth Warner Shelter, I made plans for the next couple days. Unfortunately, I have just learned from the guide book that camping is not permitted on Hell Brook where I had hoped to stay tomorrow night. Now I'm faced with a troubling choice. Being an anarchist at heart, I'm not inclined to blindly follow the rules—especially when alone in deep woods. But I'm a member of the Green Mountain Club. The GMC was created for the sole purpose of building and maintaining the Long Trail. It has tenuous relations with the private landowners, ski resorts and local governments who manage much of the land through which the trail passes. The directives outlined in the guide book help maintain those relations, thus keeping the trail open. As a GMC member, I feel obliged to do what's best for the Long Trail even if it screws up my plans. So I grumble, then adjust my plans accordingly. I can stay in the shelters a while longer, I suppose. There will be plenty of camping opportunities farther north.

As I ease down the trail, my ears catch the leaf-rustling and chatter of countless chipmunks. They are everywhere it seems. The chipmunk population has exploded recently. Where are the predators to keep them in check? Those two cold, snowy winters a short while back must have been particularly hard on coyotes and foxes. They must have burned precious calories while plowing through the white stuff during fruitless hunts. Their numbers must be down. But the past winter was a mild one. Easy living for all the forest creatures that survived, no doubt. Especially easy for those who forage, namely chipmunks and squirrels.

The balance of nature is anything but balanced. It's more like an endless series of radical shifts that only balances over extended periods of time—decades and centuries. Viewed on a much larger scale, in terms of millennia or eons, wild nature appears to be in a state of constant flux. Continents move, climates change, thousands of plants and animals come and go. How do wildlife biologists and other professional naturalists make any sense of it all? As an amateur, I am boggled by the unpredictability and complexity of the wild. There are too many factors, too many subtle relationships, too many unknown variables for me to feel comfortable saying anything definitive about it.

The Long Trail skirts an old beaver pond in the saddle between the unnamed summit and Consultation Peak. There is a little brush growing on its dam, indicating that the pond has been here a while. Yet the beaver lodge looks brand new. The water's surface is teeming with insects. An occasional wild trout swirls to the surface for an easy meal. Being an avid fisherman, I can't resist. I drop my pack then extract a telescoping fishing rod. The dragonfly resting on the decaying stump next to my pack looks fat and happy. The trout in the pond must be doing just as well.

The first few casts produce nothing. The black flies are vicious, making it difficult to concentrate on fishing. Brackish water laps towards shore. An adolescent beaver swims surprisingly close to me. I marvel at its boldness. An older beaver would be much more wary. After a few turns, the adolescent goes back to the lodge. Only then do I spot an adult working on the far side of the pond. Not paying attention to the lure on the end of my line, I snag it on a submerged branch. I loosen it with a few violent tugs then reel in my line.

Pack shouldered once again, I move steadily uphill. Puff and Shed come to mind as I reach the top of Consultation Peak. They were just about ready to hit the trail when I left them in camp this morning. Figured that they would have passed me by now. Can't help but wonder what they're doing.

Just beyond Consultation Peak, I come upon a jeep track pointing towards Sucker Pond. Another temptation. Sucker Pond would make an excellent lunch spot, I conclude after studying my maps. A few minutes later, I'm there. The perch swimming lazily in the shallows near shore discourage trout fishing, but a strong breeze from the southwest keeps the bugs away so lunch is a pleasant affair. I lounge in the rocks along the shoreline for at least an hour. Only when the grey clouds overhead threaten rain do I feel any urge to get going.

The easy trail to Congdon Camp passes through an ever-changing landscape, lending welcome variety to my walk: a cluttered forest floor beneath hardwoods, weedy wetlands, deep shade in a maturing stand of conifers. I encounter a lone, southbound hiker but decline his unspoken invitation to stop and chat. An occasional red eft brightens the damp trail. The puncheon—those hewn logs spanning the messiest mud holes like miniature footbridges—fails to keep my feet dry. It's all rotten and moss-covered, looking like it has been forgotten by local trail crews. Stamford Stream roars through the ravine immediately to my right like a Siren beckoning but I'm determined to finish the day's hike. The pack on my back grows heavier with each step. The many small stones half-buried in the eroded path torment the tender, fleshy soles of my feet.

Congdon Camp, obviously downgraded to a shelter since my guide book was last updated, materializes just as the trail turns away from the stream. The camp is nothing to rave about but I'm glad to reach it. I free my shoulders then get off my feet. Dinner is a brief affair. Afterward, I create a tidy nest for myself in one of the shelter's two top bunks. As daylight gradually fades, I'm convinced that the shelter is all mine for the evening. Just then Puff emerges from the twilight. A few steps behind him comes Shed, feet dragging and head hanging low.

"What happened to you guys?" I ask. Puff recounts their misadventures while he unpacks. Shed got into a scrape with a porcupine shortly after they left Seth Warner Shelter. Puff had to remove the quills embedded in Shed's nose—not a fun task. Immediately following that trauma, they missed a sharp turn in the trail. He and Shed spent the next six hours bushwhacking around the wilder side of Sucker Pond. Rough day. A single, deeply embedded quill still protrudes from Shed's nose like the broken shaft of a tiny arrow. Puff explains that he can't extract that one without causing Shed a great deal of pain. Darkness, intensified by a moonless sky, settles into the camp with little warning. A thick mist turns into drizzle, then becomes a steady rain as I wriggle into my sleeping bag. Within minutes it's a major downpour, complete with thunder and lightning. I whip out a flashlight and beam my food bag dangling from a tree limb thirty feet away. Then I start worrying about the four food parcels that I slung in the trees at fifty-mile intervals along the Long Trail, prior to starting this trek.

Every item of each parcel was double-wrapped in food storage bags before being placed in a larger, heavy-duty plastic bag. Then each parcel was hermetically sealed inside a plastic container or wooden box. Still, I worry. The rain is coming down in sheets. The packed earth in front of the shelter is a web of interlocking puddles. Several days will pass before I reach the first cache. Won't know until then whether or not my parcels have survived the deluge. I roll towards the shelter wall and try to forget about them. Raindrops explode loudly against the shelter's roof—a mesmerizing metallic drumbeat. Congdon Camp is watertight. Right now, that's all that matters.

Three

RED EFTS LITTER the saturated trail—bright orange spots every hundred feet or so. It's difficult to keep from stepping on them. They appear magically after a good rain, like a rainbow over the horizon. I step gingerly between them, wondering where they go when the forest turns dry. You never see them basking on sunlit rocks as their lizard cousins do. Red efts are part of the salamander family. They are newts, to be more specific. They live on land when they are young. Eventually, they return to ponds and streams to breed. During the aquatic phases of their lives, red efts are an olive drab color. On land they are bright orange—the color of unpalatable and/or poisonous things in the eyes of would-be predators. I pick one up by the tail. Its back automatically arches so that we are staring eyeball-to-eyeball at each other. Suddenly aware of the terror that must be going through its tiny brain, I put it down. I don't eat red efts but it doesn't know that. On the ground, the red eft commences a lightning crawl for cover. I watch its torturously slow, belly-dragging, torso-twisting movements. Such a bizarre success story in the annals of wild nature.

The forest is dark, wet, wearing a thin shroud of fog. The

exposed rocks along the trail are slick and moss-covered. The waterbars diverting tiny rivulets away from the trail are even slicker. I pass an old, uninhabited beaver pond. Conifers close around me during a particularly steep section of the trail, then give way to a bright green understory of young birches. Here and there along the trail, painted trilliums shine in muted light. The pink streaks on their ruffled white petals catch my eye. Mist develops into drizzle then reverts back to mist again. This is my favorite kind of day—all moist and moody. I bask in the delicious silence it affords while meandering along the trail. The only sound is that of water dripping incessantly through trees. I could wander through this dank forest all day without taking a break. The black flies and mosquitoes have been grounded by the rain, making it possible to keep a leisurely pace. My steady movement forward is virtually sweatless.

Puff and Shed are long gone. They hit the trail before I finished eating breakfast this morning. They have blasted north with youthful zeal. I don't expect to see them again. I'm hiking six miles today, only as far as Melville Nauheim Shelter. Puff hopes to travel twice that distance. And I'm sure he will, as long as he pays close attention to the white blazes.

Long before I spot them, the sweet aroma of hay-scented ferns fills my nostrils. Suddenly ferns dominate the understory. There's an openness to the woods now. Grey birches thrive among thinned maples. The ground has been blackened. There are charred stumps everywhere. A fire must have swept through here recently—not more than twenty years ago. The forest becomes a field as I crest the ridge. According to my map, this is Harmon Hill. Bennington fills the valley below. I scan the bustling city with my binoculars after dropping my pack. The faint rumble of automobile traffic filters through the forest silence. A barking dog, a chainsaw buzzing, someone yelling—sounds dislodged from their origins drift out of the valley like wayward ghosts.

A blue jay screeches noisily from a treetop, shifting my attention to more immediate surroundings. I notice the chickadees in a nearby stand of spruces. A white-throated sparrow sings, then a towhee, then a robin, then scores of songbirds that I can't quite identify. The particularly lovely warble of a small bird well-camouflaged in the nearby scrub lures me away from my slouching backpack. Next thing I know, I'm wandering aimlessly over the grassy hillside, drawn every which way by unfamiliar songs and colorful feathers flashing in the trees. A shard of light breaks through the clouds, illuminating a solitary maple. From there a finch repeats its wildly fluctuating tune. Or is it a warbler? I'm not half the birder I'd like to be. I don't have the patience that birdwatching requires, along with an eye for movement that must be quicker than thought.

Out of habit, I look at my watch—a foolish thing to do. There's no way to determine how long I've been on this hill since I don't know when I arrived. I gather up my things, then hoist the heavy load onto my back. With walking stick firmly in hand, I amble down the trail, turning wistfully at the edge of the woods for one last look at the grassy hill. How many places like this have lodged themselves in some dusty corner of my mind? More than I can enumerate. But onward I go, farther north, following deer tracks that follow the rough trail.

"Everything in nature invites us constantly to be what we are," Gretel Ehrlich writes in her book, *The Solace of Open Spaces*. As I roam through the forest along a well-marked trail, I feel something deep within me rising to the surface. The mask I wear in the lowlands is falling away. I hum the first tune that comes to mind. I drift a few yards off the trail to piss away a little excess water. The pungent smell of something rotting nearby opens the door to a more primal frame of mind—one I'd almost forgotten. How long have I been in the woods now? Long enough to recover a wilder self. I feel whole again. I become something that the plastic cards in my wallet cannot reveal. I breathe deeply, intently. I splash a little clear running water on my face as if just awakening. And the forest through which I am passing greets me with open arms. "Welcome back," it says and I'm glad to be back.

The trail drops steeply into a deep cut in the mountains where a road follows a snaking stream. I hear the roar of water and the mechanical groans of passing cars and trucks long before I step onto pavement. On the other side of the road, about fifty yards downstream from a footbridge, I nestle into a pile of rocks along the edge of the water. The sky has broken open and the sun is beating down relentlessly. The amber liquid swirling before me looks inviting. There's a deep pool in the eddy immediately to my right. I strip away clothes and immerse myself in it. The ice cold water awakens every nerve ending in my body.

A few moments later, I lounge naked on the rocks, enjoying a light lunch while drying in the sun. Someone might see me from the trail hugging the opposite side of the stream but I don't care. I slip back into my clothes only when I'm ready to pack up and go. Early afternoon already. Amazing. Melville Nauheim Shelter is still miles away.

The ascent from the road is almost as steep as the descent to it was. I immediately break into a sweat. Before going a half mile, I am wiping trickles from my brow with a sticky bandana. All too soon it's like that dip in the stream never happened. I'm hot and miserable and gasping for air like a fat tourist puffing up a volcano in the tropics. Suddenly a woman in a clean, pressed uniform bounds down the trail. Her hair is perfectly coifed. She beams pearly whites at me then says: "Happy National Trails Day!"

I must be hallucinating, I tell myself, but the young beauty blocking my way doesn't disappear when I blink. She just stands there, smiling. Next thing I know, she is chattering about the many delights of the great outdoors. She informs me that the Forest Service has freed all of its employees for the day. She and her co-workers were ordered by their bosses to head for the nearest trailheads and celebrate this unofficial holiday with guys like me. Hmm. I chug down a half liter of water, wondering what I smell like. I search the woman's face for the hint of revulsion but find only friendly eyes shimmering there. I stab the dirt with my walking stick as she tries to engage me in conversation. It's no use. I can't hold up my half of it. So we part ways. The young official wishes me a pleasant day as she skips down the trail. I face the remaining climb with weakened resolve.

A glimpse through an opening in the trees reveals a thickening haze. Hot, humid and sunbright—what a difference a few hours make! But the sky changes once again as the trail flattens out. Catching my breath, I notice the clouds gathering overhead. Two members of the Green Mountain Club coming down the trail stop long enough to give me the latest weather report: a storm is imminent. Good thing I'm less than a mile from the shelter. A light sprinkle stirs me to action but I lose momentum once it passes. No matter. I flop my gear onto the hard wooden bunk at Melville Nauheim Shelter soon enough.

The social hour begins at three. A gang of dayhikers appears at the shelter shortly after I unpack. I count twelve of them, then a couple more arrive. They're all GMC members, attending the annual club meeting at a nearby ski resort to discuss pressing issues and elect new officers. Most of them are in their thirties or older. They are impressed by my resolve to hike as much of the LT as I can. Some are envious; some have already done it; some would rather switch places with me than go back indoors and talk politics. Can't say I blame them. One grey-haired fellow asks my name, threatening to nominate me for some office. "If nominated, I will not run," I announce, "If elected, I will not serve." Then I tell a little lie about myself, just to be ornery, giving them the impression that I haven't even paid my dues this year. Suddenly, the admiring crowd transforms into a lynch mob. Thank God for the swarm of black flies arriving miraculously on a beam of sunlight! The smell of citronella and deet quickly fills the air. I suffer a couple dozen bug bites while the group mobilizes. Fortunately, the group takes most of the black flies with them when they go. Left to my own devices, I slowly ease back into a luxurious solitude.

Leaves rustle in the forest while I putter about camp. I hunker into the shadows of the shelter, slowly reaching for my binoculars as two young deer appear. They know that I'm here but don't seem to mind. They draw closer. Then there's a loud snap from the trail and the deer dart away. "Oh shit," I growl as I turn to see what spooked them.

"That's a fine greeting," an older man says to me as he steps into the clearing. He immediately drops his huge pack. Another elderly fellow appears in the next moment. I apologize, trying to explain what just happened. The two trekkers are too tired to care.

They call themselves the Pop Tarts. They are sixty-ish athletes doing the Vermont leg of the Appalachian Trail in ten days. They admit rather sheepishly that they intend to clean up and resupply at an inn in Sherburne Pass, as if that will somehow diminish the feat. Hardcore hiking such as this is utterly foreign to me. For a minute I wonder if maybe they're putting me on. Then a trio of svelte young women arrive. They call themselves the Wellesley Girls. They have a similar goal in mind. Suddenly, all five of my shelter companions are speaking some other language and I'm the odd man out—the only non-athlete in the bunch. I retreat to my nest on the top left bunk, cowering before their collective determination and physical prowess. I wallow in my slovenly, irresolute ways. A heavy rain soaks the ground in front of the shelter as everyone settles in. The shelter quickly becomes a hiker's ghetto full of dangling wet clothes and strewn gear. The congestion is downright suffocating.

Lights go out as night falls. Everyone else is prone in sleeping bags, drifting towards dreamland in no time. Everyone else is hitting the trail at the first sign of light. I lie flat on my back wondering what I'm doing here, why I've set myself up for failure by declaring myself an end-to-end hiker when I've never gone more than thirty miles at one throw. Fact is, I'm not in good enough shape to hike 260-odd miles of rugged trail. I'm no athlete by any stretch of the imagination. I'm completely out of my league. Hell, I probably won't even make it to Sherburne Pass.

Four

TRAPPED IN MY sleeping bag by lingering darkness, all I can do is lie quietly and wait for dawn. The steady drip, drip of water falling from wet clothes makes the minutes seem like hours. Everyone else is still fast asleep. Don't want to awaken them. Soon enough someone's watch alarm will go off and the shelter will be abuzz with activity. All I have to do is wait.

When morning finally comes, I waste no time getting away. I gulp down some reconstituted orange juice then hit the trail, foregoing hot coffee. I say goodbye to my shelter companions, knowing that they'll pass me on the trail in a couple of hours. No matter. I breathe a sigh of relief as I slip into the open forest. The social hour is over.

Cool, overcast dawn. I move soundlessly down the trail, having wrapped a bandana around the cooking pot inside my mess kit to muffle its rattling. Fresh deer and moose tracks cover the trail. An animal encounter is quite likely this time of day. I tread softly, keeping my senses sharpened to the prospect. Over each gentle rise, I search the forest for a glimpse of some large creature. No such luck. The Pop Tarts pass me at Hell Hollow Brook while I'm taking a break. With them in front of me, there's not much chance of seeing any wildlife. So I pick up my pace and daydream through the woods.

As the Pop Tarts and I hike along the trail, we pass each other regularly like kids playing leapfrog. Such constant contact becomes rather nerve-wracking after a while. I keep telling myself that this isn't a race but it certainly feels like one. By noon I consider taking an extended break so that the Pop Tarts can get way ahead of me. I've made good time since daybreak, having traveled seven miles already. So I drop out of the race halfway up Glastenbury Mountain. I string my mosquito bar in a patch of sunlight ten yards away from trail. The Wellesley Girls pass me a few minutes later, just as I am settling down for a long rest beneath the net.

I eat lunch while gazing at the tiny flowers dangling from the drooping stem of a modest lily called rose twisted-stalk. Suddenly I notice them all around me—hundreds of delicate pink bells ringing soundlessly at midday. I am intoxicated by their smell, as overpowering as the languid warmth of my sunny place in the woods. The steady drone of black flies and mosquitoes gathering outside the net gradually lulls me into a deep afternoon sleep.

A fire tower rises above the tall conifers atop Glastenbury Mountain. I reach it mid-afternoon, having stopped only once since lunchtime to splash stream water on my face and refill my bottles. The view from the fire tower is superb. Morning clouds have given way to afternoon blue skies. Mt. Greylock rises on the southern horizon; Green Mountain rises in the north. Mt. Equinox looms over the Vermont Valley to the northwest; Stratton Mountain stands alone to the northeast—close enough to touch. My guide book says that this is the biggest tract of roadless area in the state. It certainly seems that way. With the exception of Kelly Stand Road, half-hidden in the east/west crease immediately to the north, there are no roads in sight. Nothing but the Green Mountain National Forest spreading in all directions.

Late afternoon, a mile on the downslope of Glastenbury, I

start looking for a place to spend the night. This isn't the best ground for camping but I keep an eye open all the same. I'm not that picky. All I need is a half decent water source and a spot flat enough to lie down. Incredibly, I find water bubbling from a spring a couple hundred feet down a path leading away from a flat, cleared spot amid the chaos of fallen conifers. The cleared spot is a bit too close to the trail but it'll have to do. The steep broken terrain all around me is otherwise unsuitable. I pitch my tarp over the cleared spot and call it home for the night. The Wellesley Girls, having lingered atop Glastenbury, pass me one last time. Then I'm alone—just me, the tinkling brook and evergreen trees creaking in a soft breeze.

Three thousand feet above sea level, the forest is altogether boreal in this part of the world. An occasional yellow birch breaks the monotony of the spruce/fir canopy overhead. Not much grows in the thin film of soil underneath the conifers—moss, ferns, a few acid-tolerant plants like bunchberry and goldthread, a few wild lilies. Chipmunks seem to like it here but most other animals keep to the hardwoods at lower elevations. Moose pass through this part of the forest, on their way from one wetland to another, but they rarely linger. Bears, wildcats and coyotes often seek refuge in this high ground but they rarely show themselves. After all, they come here to avoid human contact.

This is a good place to hide out. This is an even better place to stop and listen to the wind. Occasionally, it will give away one of its precious secrets. Over the years, I've learned a thing or two from wind whispering through conifers. There's a variety of religious experience to be had only in deep woods like these. If one spends enough time alone in the boreal forest, listening carefully, one will feel the subtle yet omnipresent hand of God. There is something both comforting and terrifying about this dark, woody silence, as if good and evil have been overridden here by something much more pervasive, much more insidious. A hundred yards away from the trail in any direction, the wild is alive and well. It has all the allure of unspeakable beauty. I find myself irresistibly drawn to it.

Blaat, blaat, blaaaat!

Just when I'm beginning to feel at home in these woods, a grating noise disrupts the quiet. No wild animal makes a sound like that. It's too loud, too metallic. A few moments later, two young men on mountain bikes bounce down around a sharp bend in the trail. They're wearing t-shirts, shorts and sneakers. A single, pint-sized water bottle is affixed to the frame of each bike. That is all. No packs, no food or extra clothing. They brake hard as they roll up to me. Then one of them says: "Hi, uh, where are we?"

I stare with utter disbelief at the guy talking, then at his friend. "In the middle of nowhere," I tell them but it doesn't register. When they ask how far it is to Kelly Stand Road, I pull out my maps. It's no use. Either they haven't patience for topo maps or they simply can't read them. So I try to break it to them gently, explaining just how rough the trail ahead is going to be. They aren't listening. All they hear is: "about eight miles," which is true only if they take a critical shortcut. Confident in their ability to cycle indefinitely, they aren't the least bit concerned about the darkness slowly closing in around them. It's almost six p.m. At best, they have maybe two and a half hours of daylight left. I want to help them out but all I can do is wish them luck as they wheel away. And the sound of their bicycle horns fades into forest silence before it occurs to me that I should have offered them food, at least.

Twilight already. Time slips away quickly as I putter about camp. I fire up my cooking stove, eager to boil up water for a hot meal. The stove's blue flame flickers a few seconds before turning yellow. I try again but it does the same thing. The stove's jet is clogged so I take a tiny cleaning rod to it. The stove sputters weakly a third time, then chokes out altogether. Covered with black carbon deposits, my cooking stove needs a thorough cleaning. Should have done that before starting this trip. Haven't the time or energy for it now. What to do? There's plenty of dead wood lying about. Could start a fire easily enough but only a fool would do that in the middle of so much parched, dry kindling. Too tired, anyway. I'm ready for bed even though the sky overhead is still blue. Ten miles over Glastenbury with a heavy backpack—a full day already. So a cold dinner it is, then into my sleeping bag before the remaining light fades away.

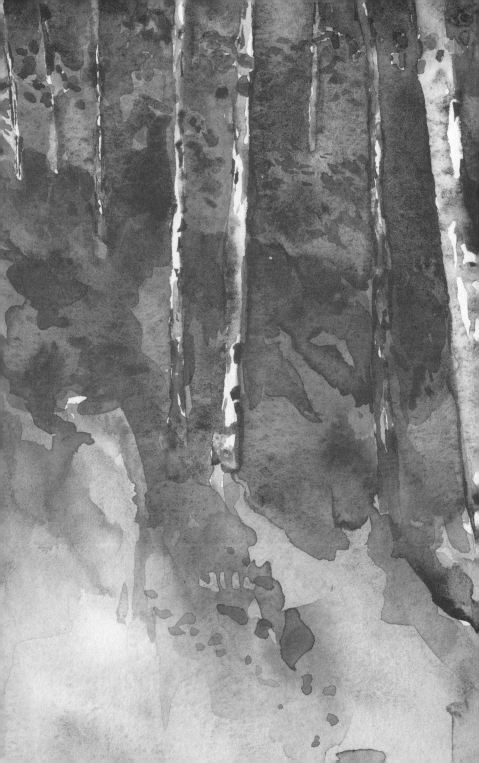

Five

As I HIKE down the trail, I can't help but wonder if all this movement is necessary. Certainly fresh air and rigorous exercise are good for one's health but is this any way to embrace wild nature? Surely it would be better to sit still, to immerse oneself in the green infinity and quietly observe. There is something unsettling about this constant rushing forward. Bagging peaks and accumulating miles seem to miss the point. Feels like I'm cheating myself. How much is being lost in this whirl of frenzied activity?

On the other hand, the regular rhythms of hiking can level the mind. Steady movement is much like a mantra chanted over and over. Steady movement reduces inner confusion and chaos the same way that white noise drowns out the invasive, distracting sounds of daily life. I immerse myself in the Eternal Present as I walk, reeling in the absolute immediacy of a trail twisting and turning through the trees. The forest opens to me. Around every bend, a new world awaits—a glimpse of some wild creature darting across the land, a beaver pond appearing unexpectedly, a rare flower blooming. There is no end to it. I savor these small, elemental surprises as the abstract concerns of a more complicated way of life gradually fade away. I become a part of the forest—a woods wanderer, a seeker of wild things, a chaser of butterflies. And the gap between self and other narrows.

"Walking is the exact balance of spirit and humility," Gary Snyder says in his book, *The Practice of the Wild*. It is the first meditation, he claims, the fusion of physical heartiness and soul. It is a marriage of mind and body that defies our conventional, dualistic interpretation of the world. Perhaps that is why I'm so troubled by it. A part of me still wants to keep mind and body in separate compartments. After all, I was raised to believe that everything has its place, that an elevated spirit lords over mere physical existence, that reason must prevail over brute impulse. Only recently has my worldview changed on this count. Slowly, reluctantly, I have become convinced that the mind isn't the alpha and omega of creation, that the corporeal world has value apart from whatever value the mind assigns to it. It's a simple concept, really—one that these woods have been teaching me for years. But sometimes it takes a great deal of backwoods wandering before a guy like me sees the obvious.

The wild runs closer to the will of God than civilization ever could. So I try to be more aware, pay closer attention, listen more carefully whenever I'm immersed in it. I may have confounded myself from the very beginning by setting out to hike the Long Trail end-to-end. In the final analysis, such a goal-oriented approach to the woods might prove to be more of a problem than movement itself. It presumes that these woods can only serve as a place to demonstrate a will to power, the triumph of the spirit or some silly concept like that. It presumes that these woods can only be good for something else. That, in turn, begs the question: What is the fundamental reason for being out here? Hmm. There are as many answers to that question as there are levels of consciousness... .

I can't really say what motivates me, first and foremost. All I can do is let things unfold as they will. Right now, it's a beautiful morning and it feels right to be panting through the forest. So enough already with the idle speculation. I hike therefore I am.

Yet another toad hops out of the path as I turn a corner. I've been seeing them all morning. This one freezes beneath a fern. I gently prod it with my walking stick, trying to get a rise out of the sluggish creature. The toad remains solid, unmoved, indifferent to me, certain somehow that it isn't on my lunch menu. It is right, of course. Still, I marvel at such steadfastness. Almost a rock, Mr. Toad is a true stoic. Time, it seems, is on its side.

I reach Story Spring Shelter shortly after high noon, putting an end to the day's hike. There are more important things to do now. As I sit munching a handful of nuts, I wonder what it would be like to eat only nuts for the next three or four days. Since my remaining food supply consists mostly of peanuts, it could come down to that. The food bag I've been carrying with me has shrunk from the size of a watermelon to a small cantaloupe. I think about the ten-pound bag of food that I slung in the trees a week and a half ago, not far from this shelter. I wonder if it is still there. I dump all my gear on the shelter floor, then go find out.

Before starting this trip, I gathered together all the food I'd need for a month on the trail. Then I divided it into six parcels. I put one of those parcels in my backpack four days ago, right before leaving the house. Another parcel is waiting for me at the post office in Jonesville, about ninety miles from the Canadian border. I mailed it there weeks ago. The other four parcels have been cached along the trail. Of those four parcels, one is inside a small plastic container dangling between two conifers, about forty miles shy of the Canadian border. The other three have been distributed across southern and central Vermont, forty to fifty miles apart. They are safe inside wooden boxes that have been slung between trees at least a hundred yards away from the trail, near shelters and/or mountain pass roads. I'll have to retrieve the plastic container way up north when I finish this hike, but the wooden boxes can be dismantled and burned along the way. That means I won't have to carry out much more than a little extra parachute cord, a handful of nails and the mosquito netting that I used to camouflage the boxes.

Before wrapping the boxes in mosquito netting, I further camouflaged them by dulling their bright wooden sides with charcoal. So now I'm just a bit concerned about finding them. This is probably a waste of mental energy. I am carrying a detailed description of each food cache's location. Besides, I'm pretty handy with a map and compass. Finding them should be child's play.

How much easier it would be to run into town and pick up what I need at a grocery store every five or six days. That's what most long-distance hikers do, enjoying a restaurant meal, a hot shower and a night in a regular bed in the process. But mine is a different approach. What I want—even more than the big brag of hiking this trail—is to spend as much time in these woods as possible without a break in the action. I'm convinced that the longer one stays in the woods, the more profound an impact the woods can have upon one's psyche. So I set up this tenuous, rather complex supply system in order to stay out here an entire month. But right now, as I slog through brushy understory on my way to the first cache, I have my doubts about the arrangement. What if one of the boxes isn't there? Then I'll have to go into town, anyway. Then all my preparation and planning would have been for nothing. No great loss, I suppose. Still, the gamble seems so ... unnecessary.

A smile breaks across my face the moment I spot the box dangling in the trees, just the way I left it. A few minutes later, I am scrambling back to the shelter with the precious supplies. After opening the box, I inspect the heavy plastic bag inside for signs of leakage. It looks okay. I dump the contents of the bag onto the shelter floor for closer inspection. To my pleasant surprise, everything is just as dry and ready to eat as it was when I packed it. No damage whatsoever, despite that deluge a few days ago. Evening alone at Story Spring Shelter. No one passed through this afternoon. No one shows up at the last minute to spend the night. A chorus of peepers rises from a beaver pond not far away. The woods around camp rustle, snap and squeak as they come alive with nocturnal activity. I am spooked by the noise until I remember that nothing particularly dangerous lurks in Vermont woods. As darkness settles over me, I lose the last of my fears in dancing flames. The dismantled box burning in the fire pit emits a great deal of heat and light. The forest around me is alive but that's okay. In lieu of human companionship, the animals make good company. I invite unseen raccoons and porcupines to dinner. I gladly dole out a few nuts to a bold chipmunk. Perhaps a big black bear will lumber out of the shadows, as amicable as an imaginary friend. Let him come.

The shelter journal is an interesting read only because I recognize so many of the people in it. The Pop Tarts pushed all the way to this shelter yesterday, ever faithful to their rigorous itinerary. The mountain bikers rolled into this camp late last night. They were utterly exhausted, hungry, dehydrated and chilled. The Pop Tarts used a cellular phone to call the local authorities. Consequently, the cyclists were extracted from the woods before midnight. The Wellesley Girls passed through here this morning, a couple hours ahead of me. They spent last night at Kid Gore Shelter, a few miles south. They hoped to cover a lot of ground today, yet they left a short note telling me how much they admire my slow-paced approach. Go figure.

Six

LOADED AND ON the trail again. I pace myself while following a winding path that gradually descends into wetlands. Toads and garter snakes move out of my way like a parting sea. I catch a whiff of rotting vegetation. A set of hoof prints scar the earth. The clumps of dried mud kicked up around the prints look incredibly fresh. There's a moose nearby. I carefully plant the tip of my walking stick with each step, avoiding the telltale sound of wood clacking against stone. I peer around each bend, over each rise, expecting to see the moose any second now. Its tracks wind through the brush, around recently downed trees. I pass beaver ponds longsince abandoned, scanning them for a dark brown silhouette. I search the shadows of a particularly thick stand of mixed birch and spruce. No moose in sight. But I can feel its presence here all the same.

Late morning. I cross Kelly Stand Road, silently congratulating myself for having hiked the first forty miles of the Long Trail. It's a personal best. I've never hiked this far before. But the Canadian border is still light years away. Can't imagine actually walking the entire trail but now I know that I'll be able to walk a good piece of it. For the first time in my life, I feel like a long-distance hiker. It's no big deal, really. Simply a matter of commitment. Simply a matter of putting one foot in front of the other, mile after mile, day after day.

A Jeep Cherokee is parked alone at the trailhead on the other side of Kelly Stand Road. There's no one in sight, though. Butterflies have gathered by the hundreds in the gravel parking lot. I've no idea why. As I walk towards a cluster of them, they take to the air. A blizzard of black and yellow wings whirls about my head. My heart flutters momentarily. The simple wingbeat movement of so many creatures is delightfully overwhelming.

Down by a stream close to the parking lot, I splash a little cold water on my face. I'd like to break for lunch and do a little fishing but the biting insects won't let me linger. A few minutes rest then it's back to the parking lot. I had hoped to leave my name in a register at this trailhead but there doesn't seem to be one. So I reenter the woods without further ado.

Now begins the long ascent up Stratton Mountain. This is the first real climb of my monthlong trek. As I climb, I recall the first time I came to this mountain, during an inaugural visit to Vermont sixteen years ago. Something happened to me then—I fell in love with this country. I felt a tremendous urge to explore every nook and cranny of it. Seven decades earlier, a schoolmaster stared at this same mountain while sitting in a nearby camp. Like me, he harbored a deep appreciation for the surrounding landscape. His name was James P. Taylor. And from his longing gaze came the inspiration to build a trail.

In March, 1910, James P. Taylor met with twenty-two other Vermonters in Burlington to create the Green Mountain Club. The sole purpose of their club was to build a single, continuous trail spanning the entire length of the state. The club's charter was designed, as Taylor put it, "to make the mountains play a larger part in the life of the people." Early that spring, as soon as the snow melted from the highlands, two of the club's members set to work. Judge Clarence Cowles and Craig O. Burt cut a three-mile section of trail from the Chin of Mt. Mansfield south to Nebraska Notch. And the Long Trail was born.

Other trail systems existed before LT, as well as other hiking clubs, but this was the first time that a group of outdoor enthusiasts had organized specifically to build a long-distance trail. Their primary goal was to blaze a pathway from Mt. Mansfield to Camel's Hump—the two mountains that dominate the Green Mountain skyline as it's seen from Burlington. A year later, that task was completed. Two years later, the trail extended all the way from Camel's Hump to Smuggler's Notch, just north of Mt. Mansfield. And Taylor's dream was on its way to becoming a reality.

When the GMC was formed, hiking was a fairly new recreational activity. No doubt it must have seemed a peculiar pastime to those who lived and worked in the woods, to those who were happy enough to hunt and fish. But the club's founders were a new breed of outdoor enthusiasts: mostly urban professionals and scholars spurred to action by the ideas of early American writers. To empire builders and newly-arrived immigrants, America was as a land that needed to be tamed. But Emerson, Thoreau and several other literary figures of the previous century looked upon it with different eyes. Theirs was an appreciation of wild nature bordering on religion. They saw something precious in the landscape, something valuable in its own right—not just raw material to make a fellow rich. The great outdoors provided a welcome counterbalance to what many of these writers considered stuffy, indoor lives. Exhilarating walks and fresh mountain air were tonics taken against the more stifling aspects of urban life. From the very beginning, hiking through the woods wasn't so much a sport as it was therapy—a temporary escape from the pressures of the so-called civilized world.

The outdoor/recreation movement came on the heels of the Industrial Revolution. Perhaps this was no mere coincidence.

The farther that humankind moves away from wild nature, the more it feels a need to reestablish some connection. But most people had other things on their minds eighty-five years ago, when the GMC was chartered. Back then, most Americans were too busy improving their standard of living to give much thought to the seemingly endless natural beauty all around them. In this respect, Taylor and his cronies were on the cutting edge of what is now a widespread movement. In their time, land preservation was a radically new idea, the National Park System was still in its infancy and the Appalachian Mountain Club—the organization that would lead to the creation of the Appalachian Trail—had not yet been established.

Atop Stratton Mountain, I encounter a GMC caretaker waiting for his co-worker to show. Our conversation is a forced affair. I am just a tad out of practice and the caretaker is obviously more at home with trees than he is with people. When the conversation diminishes to environmentalist platitudes—an assumed common ground—I hoist my pack to my shoulders and politely say goodbye. I have come to these mountains to learn the secrets of trees, rocks and running water, not to discuss politics. Besides, Stratton Pond is still several miles away. My energy is waning. The sun is sinking quickly into the western horizon. As much as I hate to admit it, I'm on the clock.

I pass another GMC worker halfway down the mountain. He is an older fellow with much better social skills and a penchant for inspiring good backcountry practices. I take mental notes during our brief chat next to a small stream. He stresses the importance of good foot care on long hikes. Then he reveals a clever method of unclogging the carbon-caked jet of my cook stove. I marvel at his wealth of trail wisdom. Before we part ways, I ask him if he would mind mailing a letter and a couple postcards for me. "No problem," he says, "Happy to do it."

Stratton Pond is a high-impact area, visited by several thousand hikers every year. The trail around the pond attests to this. It's an eroded, boggy mess wherever boardwalks and puncheon haven't been constructed. Strangely enough, there is hardly anyone at the pond right now—only me, a caretaker and a pair of overnight backpackers. As I wave away the mosquitoes and black flies swarming around my head, I ask the caretaker why no one else is here. He smiles as a sting to my cheek points out the obvious. It is early June. The insects are in their glory. Stratton Pond is an insect megalopolis.

During the half hour it takes to set up camp, the mosquitoes and flies reduce me to a feverish, trembling, slaphappy madman shouting curses. Newly-hatched deer flies circle my head, compounding the misery. Thank god for the mosquito bar! I dive beneath it after setting up my tarp. The steady drone of mosquitoes gathering at the net convinces me to eat my dinner while lying prone. It's an adequate munch. I'd rather have a hot meal but a cold one will do. Since my stove's not working, I don't really have much choice in the matter. Campfires aren't allowed at the tent sites around the pond.

After regaining my senses, I venture beyond the safety of my mosquito bar. I make a dash for the pond, keeping one step ahead of a swarm. At the water's edge, I quickly shed my clothes. Then I ease into the cold water as slowly as possible, prodded all the way by bloodthirsty bugs. Unfortunately, deer flies continue circling my head even after I'm neck-deep in the pond. I try to splash them away but they are persistent. One deer fly crashes into the pond's surface with waterlogged wings. I take note. So does the frog sitting on a rock along the water's edge. In the next moment, he's into the lake with an enthusiastic leap. Then his two amphibious eyes are level with mine. The foundering deer fly quickly disappears in a frogmouth swirl of water. I howl with delight, then shoot down another fly for my hungry friend. In a matter of minutes, the frog has a belly full of bugs and the skies immediately overhead are all clear.

A bit later, I am relatively clean and greeting the long shadows of early evening with a fresh outlook on life. Not too far off shore, the smooth surface of the pond is pocked with ever-expanding ripples. There's a feeding frenzy going on out there. I break out my fishing rod and cast a lure as far as it will go. Funny how the bugs don't seem quite as menacing now that my attention is focused upon the opportunity they've created. Wild trout fatten on the hatching insects while I, in turn, dream of fattening on them. But the trout I've already landed in my mind don't strike my lure. I should be fly fishing. My submarine temptations can't compete with the intense activity on the water's surface. All trout eyes are focused there. So I gradually lose interest, drifting along the shoreline towards the wilder side of the pond where a couple of beavers are busy working.

My half-hearted casts disrupt the beaver's twilight work. I listen to owls hooting on the other side of the pond. The sun drops from sight, leaving thick swatches of blaze orange in an otherwise pastel sky. The pond buzzes with activity as newly awakened creatures ply earth, water and sky for food and sex. The planet seethes life. I lose myself in the vernal frenzy. A stealthy mosquito sneaks away with a drop of protein-rich blood while I absently slap the place on my skin where it had landed. No apologies rendered, none accepted. So it goes. I retire to my safe-haven under the net before wild nature makes me forget how important human beings are in the greater scheme of things. All night long the teeming forest hums creation's tune. And I listen, wondering if I'm completely out of my element or back in it for the first time in a long, long while.

Seven

SKIRTING STRATTON POND on my way back to the Long Trail, I pass a couple of rundown shelters. A man and woman about my age are fixing breakfast at the second one. I stop to chat with them briefly. They're out overnight. It's an adequate back-country adventure for the woman, I gather, but the man's eyes brighten with interest when he learns that I'm out here for a month. "How's it going so far?" he asks. At the risk of sounding like a complainer, I tell him that my stove crapped out a couple days ago and I'm concerned about my dwindling supply of water purification tablets. He's surprised to hear that I'm not carrying a water filter. Who in their right mind would undertake such a journey without one? "Didn't get around to buying a filter," I say in my defense. That's a lie. Truth is, I couldn't afford one. But a week into this hike, it's clear that I should have scraped together the money somehow.

As I turn away from the overnight backpackers with "good-bye" rising to my lips, the man pulls an unopened bottle of water purification tablets out of his pack. At first I reject the gift, feeling a little sleazy for having driven him to such generosity. He insists, assuring me that he only carries them in case of emergency. I take the tiny bottle in hand. It feels like gold as I roll it back and forth in my palm. I thank the man a half dozen times, then thank him again before departing with a lottery winner's smile on my face. My spirit soars as I race along the trail. The small bottle of tablets guarantees drinking water for another hundred miles. But this sudden turn of good fortune isn't enough by itself to sustain such a brisk pace. A mile and a half down the trail, a mounting ache in my joints slows me down. A week on the trail and I'm feeling it. Spruce Peak Shelter is only a few miles farther north. It's a sweet place, I've been told. Will rest up there for a day or so before continuing north.

The path underfoot turns westward. A light drizzle comes and goes. The trail widens into a woods road, hugging the northeastern edge of the Lye Brook Wilderness before it descends gradually towards the city of Manchester. Signs posted along the left side of the road warn against the hazards of travel in the wilderness area beyond. It takes all the will power I can muster to stay on the road. The wildman in me wants to abandon this gentle pathway and dive into the beckoning, untrammeled forest. I resist the urge, knowing that I'll have ample opportunity to go in there some other day. Right now, the main thing is to stay on task, following the white blazes stretching north. Just this once I'm going to move through the woods the way most people do: keeping to the trail with a specific goal in mind. Plenty of time for aimless wandering later.

"There is no wilderness as such left in New England," Edward Hoagland once declared in a long essay on the subject. I know exactly what he means by that. Like Hoagland, I've been to that wide-open country in the northwestern corner of the continent. I have spent time in *real* wilderness. I know what it's like to go days without seeing anything even remotely human. But here in New England, it's difficult to hike more than a dozen miles in any direction without crossing a road.

When Thoreau and his ilk ventured into Northern New England a hundred and fifty years ago, it was a country as wild and dangerous as Alaska is today. But there has been a great deal of human intrusion here since then. Hoagland is right in the strictest sense. This land has been tamed. All the same, a pocket of undeveloped country like the Lye Brook Wilderness can be a good place to escape the cacophony of modern society. Small pockets of wilderness like this aren't to be underestimated. One can get pleasantly lost in them.

Roaming about wilderness areas teaches one a great deal about what it means to be human—much more than a course in philosophy or anthropology ever could. After all, the wild is where we came from. The wild is as much a part of our nature as the most fundamental aspects of civilization. Nowadays we are only visitors to roadless areas, it's true. But once there was no difference between wilderness and the place we called home.

Just beyond the Lye Brook Wilderness, I come upon Prospect Rock—an exposed outcrop overlooking Manchester. Time for an extended break. A young, rather sad-looking fellow is lounging on the rock. I cautiously disrupt his solitude, hoping that he doesn't mind. Turns out that he welcomes the chance to talk about what's troubling him. He has recently been charged with dealing drugs at a rock concert and is now awaiting trial. He's certain that the judge will send him to the nearest state prison—not a pleasant prospect for anyone, much less a twenty-ish fellow who loves the great outdoors. While the young man is telling me all this, I notice the strange device strapped to his ankle. At a preliminary hearing, the judge determined that the young man was a flight risk. Consequently, an electronic signaling device was put on his leg in order to keep him tethered to the legal system. "It's not so bad," the young man tells me, "Without it, I'd still be sitting in jail." This way, at least, he can dayhike to beautiful places like Prospect Rock. All the same, I find it difficult to share the young man's optimism. I take a long hard look at the little black box and thank God that I don't have something like that strapped to me.

When the young man asks where I'm headed, I'm reluctant to say. In the shadow of his misfortune, my freedom seems an obscene luxury. But the young man smiles when I confess that I'm backpacking all the way to Canada. "You're on the righteous path," he says, as if my hike somehow mirrored a lifestyle choice. I flatly deny it, telling him that I'm just lucky enough to stay in the woods for a while. The fellow babbles something about how I've escaped The Great Babylon. I'm skeptical of such pseudo-religious proclamations but take advantage of his inflated opinion of me. I ask him to do me a favor. He accepts my small bag of trash with a broad smile. He considers it divinely appropriate—returning waste to a civilization that has become a spiritual wasteland.

I thank the young man, then get up and walk away. A tear wells in the corner of my eye for reasons I can't quite fathom. I follow the white-blazed trail splitting away from the woods road that descends to Manchester. I press north, thinking about that thing on his ankle, thinking about all the wild animals I've seen on tv nature shows with radio collars around their necks. Wildlife management, hmm... Social order, yes, but at what cost?

What a pleasant surprise! Spruce Peak Shelter isn't just a shelter. It's an enclosed cabin, newer and cleaner than most. There's a good spring nearby and an excellent view of the Valley of Vermont from a clearing only a minute away. Not to mention a compost toilet—that backwoods amenity on the cutting edge of environmentally sound technology. The reports I heard about this shelter were understated. I waste no time making myself comfortable, spreading my gear across a lower wooden bunk inside. This is a perfect place to rest up.

No one joins me. I savor a long, delicious solitude while enjoying the small pleasures of a well-kept camp. A field mouse scratches somewhere beneath the floor. A strange silence envelopes the forest at dusk—no peepers, no crickets, no owls, no wind or leaves rustling. Just me and a rummaging mouse who ignores my thumping protests. The constant scratching noise reverberates through the shelter's rustic vaults. I manage to sleep well, anyway.

In the morning, I eat breakfast on the porch as an all-day rain commences. Then I go about my business: washing clothes, writing letters, getting my stove up and running again. In the afternoon, I'm awakened from a short nap by the sudden appearance of a lone backpacker. He's a soft-spoken, silver-haired gentleman who has hiked here from a nearby trailhead to spend the night. Not too far behind him is a party of three: two young men calling themselves Plum and Mustard and a rather talkative woman. They roll into camp just as the rain stops. Like me, Plum and Mustard are aspiring end-to-enders. Their previous backwoods experience is limited to a few short trips but they are psyched for the long hike to Canada. The young woman accompanying them is going only as far as the next mountain pass road. She determined beforehand that a week on the trail would be plenty. She looks forward to being clean again.

When the silver-haired gentleman invites me to join him for a Cajun rice dinner, complete with fresh asparagus, I don't have to ponder the matter very long. I seize the opportunity to escape my steady diet of dried food—one as bland as it is repetitive. The asparagus is straight from his garden. Can't remember the last time I ate anything so tasty. I thank him repeatedly. When he offers to take my mail to Manchester, I can hardly believe it. I wrote a rather important letter to Judy just this morning, asking her to ship a stove maintenance kit and another bottle of water purification tablets to Jonesville for me. The silver-haired gentleman says he could put the letter in a mailbox tomorrow. My good fortune continues. With the help of generous dayhikers and overnight backpackers, I just might be able to stay in these woods after all.

Eight

THE THERMOMETER ON the shelter porch reads 40 degrees at dawn. Tiny clouds of vapor materialize with each breath. Breakfast is a brief affair. I pack up my things like a fugitive driven by hounds baying in the distance. After a full day's rest, I charge towards a mountain pass road a couple miles away. Crossing the road requires a certain degree of wariness. Sleepy commuters sip coffee from thick plastic mugs while racing past in noisy machines. I slip across the road, then begin a steady ascent. I'm halfway up Bromley Mountain before the sun clears the trees. On top by midmorning.

The grassy slopes of Bromley are abandoned. The lift is idle and the ski hut is boarded up. I am strangely alone in this mountaintop ghost town. There are people in the ski village a mile below but no sound comes from that direction. I climb the observation deck, hoping to catch a breeze that'll keep the bugs out of my face for a short while. A cold wind stirs out of the west. Grey clouds droop from the sky like rumpled sheets. The landscape beneath them is a patchwork of dark forest shadows and luminescent treetop verdure. The cheery disposition of an open meadow in the distance diffuses the sky's somber mood.

Visibility is remarkably good despite the clouds overhead. I spot Greylock way to the south, Killington far north, Mt. Ascutney eastward. The Taconics rise dramatically out of the Valley of Vermont to the west. Beyond them, a vague blue outline suggests the Adirondacks. Half of Vermont spreads before me—a turbulent sea of green waves frozen in geologic time. I feel empowered, jubilant, lucky to be alive. Suddenly I understand what Ethan Allen meant when he said: "The gods of the hills are not the gods of the valleys." We who call these mountains home have an affinity with the wild that surpasses any allegiance to lowland society. In every wild heart there's a rascal who won't play by the rules, a quiet anarchist who feels compelled to live by a higher law. The Green Mountains teem with restless souls like mine, as all mountain ranges do. The mountains themselves encourage a passion for absolute freedom.

The descent goes quickly. I eat lunch in Mad Tom Notch, basking in unexpected sunshine at midday. A pump just beyond the parking lot in the notch provides ample drinking water. Trusting the source, presumably a deep well, I drink from it without giving much thought to giardia or any other health hazard. I did the same at Spruce Peak Shelter. Hmm... Developing a bad habit—one that could eventually force me off the trail. With great reluctance, I toss a couple iodine tablets into my refilled water bottle. Since I don't want my bowels churning with parasites, I'll play it safe from now on.

Just beyond Mad Tom Notch, I enter Peru Peak Wilderness. It's a small pocket of undeveloped land in the middle of the Green Mountain National Forest. Entering this wilderness feels like a homecoming. For the first time since I started this hike, I don't have to think about who owns the land and what I can or cannot do on it. A simple joy stirs within.

Deep in this small wilderness area, between Styles and Peru Peaks, the forest is distinctly boreal: evergreen, boggy and inhospitably wild. Snowshoe hares spy on me from the cluttered understory, darting away whenever I get too close. A set of deer prints pressed deep into the muddy trail suggest that other eyes might be watching me as well. Black flies gather about my head, excited by the prospect of a walking meal. A sweet rotting smell permeates the forest. Bright white bunchberry flowers are abundant. There's no indication that any other hikers have passed this way lately, though I'm sure they have. No matter. Today this is my wilderness.

My knees complain on the downslope of Peru Peak, urging me to make camp soon. Peru Peak Shelter isn't more than a mile away, just beyond the wilderness boundary, but it won't do. If I stay there, I'll have company tonight. Not in the mood for it. So I start looking for a place to set up my tarp.

I stumble upon a tiny stream just as conifers give way to hardwoods. It lures me several hundred yards away from the trail, to a rather flat piece of ground beneath an ancient fir. The thick forest duff underfoot will make a good bed, so I stretch my tarp over the spot after tying back the surrounding hobblebush. Dinner is expedient—ramen noodles boiled in minutes on the stove. I want to get under my tarp as soon as possible. The fading twilight creates a sense of urgency and the mosquitoes are especially menacing. Besides, I'm tired after thirteen miles of trail. I slip under the net dangling from the tarp, going back outside only once to piss away what little water didn't turn into sweat this afternoon. A pileated woodpecker laughs insanely from the upper branches of a mighty birch, reminding me that I'm not alone. I laugh right back at him, then abandon all concern to the loud gurgle of water trickling over rocks.

Slip knots. The fastest way to break camp in the morning is to secure each and every line with a looped knot the night before. That way they can be easily undone. Slip knots require a little extra effort, a little thinking ahead. Over the years, the backcountry traveler endures a number of hardships. Alone in the wild, memories resurface to prevent him or her from making the same mistakes twice. Slip knots in guylines, in clotheslines, in the cord holding up food bags—the faster one can break camp, the better. Slip knots reflect a primal fear of the unknown, a healthy respect for the wild. A terrible storm could develop overnight. Air temperatures could drop well below freezing in the early morning hours. Or one could awaken with a spiking fever. Best to be able to move quickly when dawn comes.

In the lowlands, stability is the ideal. We create rigid routines for ourselves, tying our lives with knots that do not come apart without a great deal of effort. But the wilderness must be approached differently. Wilderness experiences should always have slip knots in them—quick releases enabling the traveler to adapt to ever-changing circumstances. Everything out here is fluid, mobile, indeterminate. The natural world is more chaos than order. The determinist is caught unaware by the unknown; the mystic anticipates it and loops his knots accordingly. Wilderness is unforgiving to those who rely upon reason alone. Be ready for sudden changes in the wind; pay attention to omens. The spirit of the wild appears the very moment one is most vulnerable, when things aren't completely under control. The knot tied too securely binds one to a rational arrogance, to logical demise. Slip knots anticipate unforeseen events, allowing one to go with the flow. Pull the cord and let it all unravel... or stay in the lowlands where things are much more predictable.

Morning overcast, windy, rain threatening. I break camp in a hurry, then return to the trail feeling just a little bit wilder. An easy twenty-minute walk gets me to Peru Peak Shelter. Surprisingly enough, the shelter is empty. Could have had the place to myself last night. No matter. My off-trail bivouac was a much needed break from the routine. I'm more comfortable out here now. I belong in this forest now—no longer just passing through.

Moose tracks once again, in the bottomlands between Peru Peak Shelter and Griffith Lake. I stray from the trail, following a set of fresh tracks into alders and willows before realizing just how futile this stalk is going to be. The moose are much more familiar with the alder bush than I am. It'll be nearly impossible to catch them unaware in here. Better to sit at a major intersection of moose tracks and wait. But no, I don't have the patience for that. Not today, anyhow.

The puncheon along the eastern edge of Griffith Lake makes for easy walking. I get a good head of steam going and am tempted to blast north at full speed. But there's no reason to rush. Going only seven miles today. So I stop and cast a line into the lake, despite choppy water and spitting clouds. Once again the casting ritual is just an excuse to pay attention. I throw lures into the lake until my ears and eyes take their fill of water lapping against a rocky shore. Then I move on.

The trail arcs northward into Big Branch Wilderness, gently meandering through open woods. Then it gradually eases uphill towards Baker Peak. I take lunch amid the exposed rocks of Baker's summit while watching a squall creep up the Valley of Vermont like a translucent, fast-moving glacier. Already Manchester has been consumed by it. A glasslike sink called Emerald Lake is next. I hurry through the rest of my lunch, then quit the exposed rocks before the storm reaches me.

The long descent to Big Branch Shelter is delightful. The rocky trail becomes a grassy woods road, giving my eyes a welcome break from the constant search for good footing. I pass a lone dayhiker, then a troop of a GMC members. They are on their way to Lost Pond in search of pitcher plants. No doubt their quest will be fruitful. They've selected the right time and place. Wouldn't mind joining them but I have more practical matters to consider.

About two and a half weeks ago, I slung box number two in the trees about a quarter mile west of Big Branch Shelter. While cruising down the trail, I can't help but wonder if that cache has survived the past couple weeks of storms. I wonder if it has been disturbed by wild animals or by one of the many outdoor enthusiasts who frequent this wilderness area. My pace quickens as I think about it. Even though I still have a two- or three-day supply of food on me, I'll have to tap that cache in order to stay on the trail all the way to Brandon Gap. Hardly what you'd call a dire situation but I'm anxious all the same.

At Big Branch Shelter, I perform the peanut-eating ritual while anticipating the worst. Can't imagine living on nuts alone for much more than a day. They are fast becoming my least favorite food. I packed too damned many of them this trip. If box number two is disturbed, then I'm headed for the nearest town to resupply. That's all there is to it.

I tramp into the woods without checking my notes. It's been a while since I was here last but I remember the route as if I'd walked it yesterday. A few minutes into the bushwhack, I spot the dangling box and all's well with the world. But one small detail prevents an outburst of self-congratulation. The parachute cord that keeps the box suspended in the air is frayed where it has rubbed in the crotch of a supporting tree. Hadn't even considered the possibility of cord being worn thin by friction. Hmm... Brandon Gap is a week away. The next box could be on the ground by the time I reach it.

Nine

BIG BRANCH SHELTER is in sorry shape. A couple of floor boards are missing. The ground around the fire pit is hard-packed and charred. There is trash everywhere. Some damned fool busted up the picnic table and used it for firewood, so now there are half-burnt remnants of it strewn all over the place. This shelter is only a mile away from a major trailhead. Consequently, it gets the worst kind of use. A group of dayhikers left the remains of their lunch in a garbage bag hanging on a nail, no doubt assuming that a trash collector would come along to pick it up. In this particular case, the trash collector is me. I fill the garbage bag with all the other trash scattered about the shelter, then set it aside. When the GMC group returns from their Lost Pond excursion, I ask them if they'd carry it out. They're not enthusiastic about the prospect but they understand the situation. Since I'm not the one who created the mess, I refrain from apologizing. After they leave, I do what little else I can to tidy up the shelter grounds. Then I attend to my own affairs.

It is Saturday and this particular section of trail is a hiker's highway. Two backpackers pass through camp, then a lone day-hiker. A leggy jogger breezes by nonchalantly as if doing laps on a track. A long-distance hiker flops into the shelter to catch his breath before continuing south. He is disheveled and tired-looking. His shirt is a patchwork of brown, grey and yellow stains. I offer him a pepperoni stick after he complains about a powerful fat craving. He accepts the gift reluctantly. Like most so-called athletes on this trail, he's packing nothing but carbohydrates. He frowns at the fatty substance in hand as if it has been made by the devil himself. I suppress a grin. We trade information about shelters and water sources, then he's on his way—ever faithful to a grueling twenty-mile-a-day itinerary. I wish him luck even though I don't quite understand why he's punishing himself.

As evening draws nearer, a pair of backpackers appear from the south. They claim the empty space next to me in the shelter. They, too, are trying to hike the entire LT at one shot. Their trail names are Husky and Mr. Clean. Husky got his tag from an exhausted fellow hiker who thought Husky should pull him along a snow-covered trail like a sled dog. The tag stuck. Mr. Clean looks like the character on the bottle of household cleaner that goes by the same name. There is only a week's worth of fuzz on his otherwise clean-shaven head.

When Husky and Mr. Clean ask for my trail name, I tell them to call me Raven. I spent a couple weeks alone in the wilds of Southeast Alaska a few years back. Whenever I got into a hairy situation out there, a raven would suddenly appear. Since then, I've felt an affinity with that bird. Granted, mine is a rather humorless, unimaginative trail name but it'll have to do. After hearing some of the less-than-flattering names that other hikers have acquired on the trail, I've concluded that it's best to name yourself before someone else does. The trail has its own subculture, as a quick perusal of any shelter log reveals. The best names are funny ones but trail humor often leaves something to be desired.

While Husky and Mr. Clean are making themselves at home in the shelter, I exchange food, stories and information with them. Mr. Clean and I covet each other's granola bars, so we do a swap. To lighten my increasing burden of peanuts, I offer a one-pound bag to my shelter companions. Mr. Clean takes the bag, then gives me a set of fresh batteries. Good trade. Extra batteries are a detail that I'd overlooked while packing for this trip. My flashlight is dim already. As we pull out our maps, we talk about the only other northbound end-to-enders we've encountered so far: Plum and Mustard. Last seen, they were waiting at a mountain pass road for someone to bring them fresh supplies. Husky and Mr. Clean passed them yesterday. Husky figures that Plum and Mustard must have reached Griffith Lake by now. I might see them tomorrow.

Daytrippers disappear as evening unfolds. Husky, Mr. Clean and I sit around the fire pit, watching my wooden box go up in flames while we eat dinner. The steady roar of the nearby stream overpowers the more subtle sounds of the night forest. Together fire and water have a hypnotic affect. We are drowsy in no time.

In the morning, we awaken to steady rainfall. My shelter companions sink into a funk. I, on the other hand, am delighted by the prospect—much preferring a walk in the rain to swarming insects. I take to the trail in a flash, hiking faster than usual. The rain keeps me nice and cool.

At Little Rock Pond, I stop to watch the dance of water vapor extending down from low clouds. The rain tapers to a fine mist. Husky and Mr. Clean shoot past, setting a comfortable pace for themselves. Eventually, I follow them up the trail. At the northern end of the pond, I run into a large group of teenagers on a high school outing. They are headed for my intended destination: Greenwall Shelter. This precipitates a change of plans. I'll push all the way to Minerva Hinchey Shelter instead of stopping at Greenwall. I charge through the teenagers, into the quiet forest beyond their incessant chatter. When I catch up with Husky and Mr. Clean, I give them the news. They don't seem to mind. They, too, are headed for Minerva but welcome my company for another night. We leapfrog down the trail a couple more times before they dart ahead. I slow down considerably just beyond Greenwall. With a thirteen-mile hike on my plate today, I'd better pace myself.

The poorly maintained section of trail down to Wallingford Road has been turned into a runoff stream by this morning's rain. My boots are completely soaked and muddy after a half mile of it despite my best rock-hopping efforts. The guide book says that this particular section of trail will soon be rerouted. That explains why it has been neglected. All the same, I resent the slippery descent. It's no fun at all. Such a relief to finally reach Wallingford Road! From there it's an easy walk up a dirt road to Minerva.

Minerva Hinchey Shelter is full of dripping clothes and muddy gear by the time Husky, Mr. Clean and I settle into it. Fortunately, no other backpackers come along to compound the mess. A moose calls from nearby wetlands at dusk. We go down to investigate but aren't lucky enough to spot the huge, lumbering animal. A bat squeaks from its nest in the shelter rafters. The rabies warning plastered to the shelter wall sets all three of us on edge but the young bat stays put. Soon enough a steady rain lulls us to sleep.

In the morning I loaf about the shelter, giving Husky and Mr. Clean a good head start. I'm sure they don't like leapfrogging any more than I do. They depart right before I finish breakfast. As soon as they are gone, a deep silence emerges from the dripping trees. I meander down the wet, foggy trail later on, happy to be moving through such a mysterious world—all shadowy conifers and mist. My walking stick finds the slick muddy spots in front of me. A light wind lifts the fog from the trees as I grope towards Clarendon Gorge. Virginia waterleaf is the flower of the day. The protruding stamens of its white, bell-like flowers point every which way.

The footbridge across the gorge is a sturdy structure but the white water roaring through the rocks far below intimidates me all the same. I do not linger on the span. The bridge is dedicated to a hiker who died in this gorge—yet another reminder that even a simple walk like this isn't entirely risk-free. I tighten the shoulder straps of my backpack as if to gird myself against carelessness, then continue north. Crossing the nearby road, I give passing motorists plenty of leeway, sensing the tremendous difference between their pace and mine.

The fallow field on the other side of the road is full of tall grass and wildflowers: clover, buttercup, chickweed, dewberry, daisy fleabane and hawkweed. It's the first true sign of summer. The patch of buttercups I spotted in the woods a couple days ago seemed more springlike somehow. As the seasons change, the bloom migrates from dark forest to open field. The Summer Solstice is only a week or two away. The migrating bloom reminds me that my hike can't go on forever. I make a quick calculation and surprise myself. I've been on the trail twelve days already.

Ten

SHORTLY AFTER REENTERING the woods, I struggle up a rain-soaked, rocky trail that looks more like a stream bed than anything else. I stop for lunch at Clarendon Shelter, a half mile beyond the steep incline, having earned a rest. Drizzle thickens to rain. I break out my stove, glad to have a roof over my head for the occasion. The stove sputters and hisses but I am able to boil up enough water for a cup of tea. Blue jays keep me company. They screech from the wet tree branches nearby, oblivious to the rain. No one else is foolish enough to be out right now. I lay a few peanuts near a chipmunk burrow. Nothing happens. Time passes while I daydream. A glance at my watch urges me to pack up and get going. I've lingered at this shelter well over an hour—long enough for the rain to run its course.

The trail beyond Clarendon Shelter is a good mix of field and forest—ideal country for ruffed grouse. I spook nesting families of them every hundred yards or so. Time and again, a surprised hen plays out the broken wing ruse to distract me while her chicks fly away. The first time a grouse flaps about the forest floor with mock cries, I am enthralled. But the routine wears thin after a while. "Enough already!" I shout, after seeing the performance a half dozen times. The next hen throws herself into the act with all the enthusiasm she can muster. I shrug off the demonstration, wishing that ruffed grouse could somehow expand their repertoire.

The trail crosses a dirt road, then points towards Killington—the 4,000-foot mountain that I'll be climbing tomorrow. The trail follows a small stream that looks like brook trout water. I consider stopping and trying to fish it but the heaviness in my legs urges me forward. I'm tired. Yesterday's long hike took more out of me than I thought. Or perhaps it's just the cumulative effect of so many days on the trail. Either way, I have no energy this afternoon. I drop my pack then sit on a rock to rest. I am carrying too much weight—that's for certain. Too much food; way too many nuts. It's time to find some hungry chipmunks or squirrels.

"Hello," someone says.

I nearly fall off the rock. Looking up I see a tall, thin man standing calmly before me. No idea how he got there. "Hello," I say right back. Eyeballing the man's small rucksack, I add, "Out for the day, are you?"

"No, I'm going to Harper's Ferry."

"West Virginia?" I respond skeptically. He nods his head. Upon closer inspection, I can see that this is no ordinary man standing in front of me. A wild-eyed, forty-ish fellow toughened by hundreds of miles of rugged terrain, he's obviously a seasoned AT hiker. All skin, muscle and gristle. Wandering Oak, he calls himself. Bona fide trail junkie, traveling ultra light. Not an ounce of excess weight on him anywhere—not in his pack or on his bony frame. One of those mythical creatures I'd heard about but hadn't encountered, until now.

As if to convince me that he's telling the truth, Wandering Oak opens his pack to show me a complete though remarkably compact outfit: a rain parka that fits comfortably in the palm of his hand, a first aid kit in a sandwich bag, a food bag the size of a grapefruit, etc. Says he can hike five days on that much food. Yeah, right. No wonder he's so thin. Yet I admire him. He's the wizened trail Buddha while I'm a mere novice, muddling blindly towards one-hundred-mile enlightenment. He floats over the trail while I pound the rutted path deeper into the ground. But admiration sours to envy, then to outright resentment as I shoulder my immense load. Out of sheer spite, I'd like to saddle the guy with a two-pound bag of nuts. But no, he's too smart to accept it. Besides, the encounter doesn't last long enough for me to even attempt a hand-off. Wandering Oak isn't one to stand about idly very long. After zipping up his pack, he says goodbye then scoots down the trail with absurd ease. I lumber in the opposite direction, groaning uphill, wondering if maybe I should leave long-distance hiking to those who are better suited for it.

A short while later, I see things in a different light. It occurs to me that the longer one stays out here, the more of an outsider one becomes. Take Wandering Oak out of the woods and what do you have? Can't imagine him being anything but a street bum back in the lowlands. Hiking isn't the only thing I do, thank god. I have a life beyond these trees. But who knows? Maybe he does, too. Maybe Wandering Oak is a computer scientist, a stock broker or a corporate lawyer in his other life. You never know.

I reach Governor Clement Shelter late afternoon. Husky and Mr. Clean have the place looking like a squatter's camp already. With clotheslines strung everywhere, the derelict shelter has all the charm of a hillbilly shack. I make some rude comment about the decor, then drop my pack. Husky ignores me. He has a radio plastered to his ear, hoping to hear some encouraging news about tomorrow's weather. Mr. Clean introduces me to a couple of the many bold chipmunks overrunning the place. He protests loudly when I toss a few nuts to the varmints. He insists that I'm only making matters worse. I don't care. I have too many nuts and don't feel like hauling them all up Killington tomorrow. Desperate situations call for desperate measures.

After settling into camp, I fire up my cook stove. It sputters, flickers, then goes out. I've been here before. I try unclogging the stove's jet and firing it up again. The stove wheezes and coughs one last time before bursting into a dysfunctional orange flame. So I shut the stove down, declaring it disabled. There should be a stove maintenance kit waiting for me in Jonesville by now, assuming that Judy got my letter. But Jonesville is still ninety miles away. That means a week's worth of campfires and/or cold meals—a rather grim prospect. Or I could say to hell with staying in the woods and head for the nearest town tomorrow morning. Such a digression wouldn't take me away from the trail for much more than a day. Hmm. Tough choice.

Mr. Clean and Husky offer the use of their stove for the night but I'm too damned proud to accept it. My own stove or nothing. So I retreat to my sleeping bag to brood. Every outdoor adventurer has his or her tales of equipment failure but it seems like I have more than my share. Should have brought a maintenance kit with me. Should have planned better. Oh well. Nothing can be done about it now.

Eleven

RISING TO THE challenge, I leap from bed and start gathering
sticks. Then I build a fire. It's a frustrating task since the wood is
still damp from yesterday's rain but I'm on a mission now. I blow
on the smoky fire while painstakingly inserting sticks into it,
nursing along flickering flames for the better part of an hour.
Husky and Mr. Clean watch curiously as they drift through their
regular morning routine. They don't understand why I don't just
make a trip into town for a stove maintenance kit. Life would be
so much easier that way. They pack up their things and leave. I'm
relieved by their departure, happy to finish the task without an
audience. But when the sticks burn smokeless and flames dance
joyously in the clear morning air, I wish there was someone
around to witness it.

Late start. On the trail mid-morning, I steel myself against
the long Killington ascent. It's a great mound of rock and earth
thrusting upward—just a taste of what's to come. I set a steady
pace and am standing on top of Killington a few hours later,
wondering how I missed the hard part. Aside from the last quar-
ter-mile scramble, the climb wasn't bad at all.

On the rocky summit, a slight breeze cools me down while I

enjoy the hazy view. Black flies take full advantage of the rare interludes between gusts of wind. Otherwise they don't pose much of a problem. A young couple suddenly appears a few yards away, dressed in tennis shoes and clean, white clothes. They have just walked up a grassy ski slope from the nearby lodge. They're in love, so I graciously relinquish the summit to them. Right before leaving, though, I ask if they'd mind mailing a few postcards for me. No problem, they say. So I hand-off a small packet before disappearing.

In the saddle between Killington and Pico, I blindly follow the trail, letting my mind wander. I spot a painted trillium arising from the detritus on the forest floor. The pale flower is only a ghost of its former self. Its delicate white petals have become translucent with age. Spring is only a fading memory now. A mounting summer heat bakes away the last of any snowmelt dampness still lingering beneath the trees.

I reach Pico Camp with several hours of daylight remaining. Short hike today. Burned enough calories getting up Killington Peak. No need to kill myself. Besides, I've heard good things about this camp and look forward to spending a little time here. Will probably have the place all to myself, now that Husky and Mr. Clean are ahead of me. A note in the shelter journal reaffirms what I already suspect: they have continued hiking to Sherburne Pass where they intend to hitch a ride into town. Will probably run into them on the other side of the pass. Then again, maybe not. Nothing out here is written in stone.

Pico Camp is a humble cabin thirty-four hundred feet above sea level, built into the side of Pico Peak. The grassy clearing in front of it affords a good view eastward, looking over Killington ski village. Mt. Ascutney looms on the horizon directly ahead, about forty miles away. I search the northeast skyline for the White Mountains but can't find them. There is a cloudbank in the way. A nearby trickle of water tinkles in the dark, evergreen forest.

While gathering wood, I catch a glimpse of a snowshoe hare hopping through the shadows. As dusk settles over the mountain, I reconstitute a freeze-dried dinner before a fire burning steady in front of the cabin. A snowshoe hare, sporting its brown summer coat, cautiously moves into the clearing from the wood's edge. Another appears a few minutes later. Good company. Together we eat our evening meals—their fibrous munching punctuated by my noisy slurps. A slate-colored junco cries loudly from the top of a spruce, then all is quiet. And the azure sky overhead deepens to cobalt blue as the sun sets on the other side of the mountain.

The resort below is a constellation of lights shining in eerie calm. The luminous edge of the eastern cloudbank anticipates a full moon rising into newborn darkness. My fire diminishes to a volcanic glow. I go inside the cabin, drawn there by fatigue, leaving the hares to finish their browse without me. I watch for the moon through the cabin window, listening to a solitary mosquito whine at the dirty glass pane.

"The infinite bustle of nature on a summer's noon, or the infinite silence of a summer's night, gives utterance to no dogma," Thoreau once wrote in his journals. Tonight, Pico Camp is consumed by that silence and I am only a watchful set of eyes and ears. My thoughts are muffled by the absolute authority of an ineffable calm. What can one conclude from such stillness? Only that it is best to lie quietly in one's sleeping bag and let it reign. The moon flashes brilliantly over the cloud's edge, then climbs into full view in the purple sky like the unblinking eye of God itself. The inside of the cabin is awash in moonlight. A silhouetted mouse scurries across the table, then rifles through my things. My eyelids become leaden as I stare back at that great white orb filling the window. Then I fall asleep.

In the morning, it's an easy walk to Sherburne Pass where I cross the road between speeding cars. Then I sneak back into the forest.

Moving too fast, a gentle climb has me hyperventilating. But soon enough I've beaten the grade and am staring at a fork in the trail. To my right, the Appalachian Trail continues east towards New Hampshire. To my left, the Long Trail veers north towards the Canadian border, through the rest of the Green Mountain State. Hard to believe that I've hiked a hundred miles already.

I turn left, knowing that the fun is just beginning. The trail will become more rugged now. There are at least a dozen major mountains still ahead—any one of which is a full day's hike in its own right. With a heavy pack tugging at my shoulders, I have my work cut out for me. But, according to my maps, the next ten or fifteen miles of trail are relatively flat. So I'll take advantage of the situation and cover as much ground as possible between now and dusk.

Mid-afternoon, I stop at Rolston's Rest. Husky and Mr. Clean have claimed the shelter already. After an overnight visit to the lowlands, they are happy enough to lounge about camp for the remainder of the day, enjoying newly acquired delicacies. Husky presents me with the box of snack crackers that I'd asked him to pick up for me. I tear into the package like a starving wolf, inhaling handfuls of crackers between gulps of water. All fired up now, I'm ready for a late afternoon hike. I feel great but Husky and Mr. Clean wonder if perhaps my judgement has been impaired by too much time alone in the woods. No matter. I am hellbent upon hiking as much as I can today. We make tentative arrangements for a shelter rendezvous tomorrow evening, then part ways.

Twelve

ENTHUSIASM QUICKLY DISSIPATES as the stroll past Chittenden Reservoir becomes a forced march along an unimproved, overgrown path. According to my map, the trail hugs contour lines for well over three miles. I soon find out otherwise. It's a roller coaster ride, a long succession of 100-foot elevation changes that some cartographer overlooked. But the cartographer isn't the only one at fault here. There's no reason for the trail to rise and fall this way. Whoever blazed this section of the LT obviously lacked common sense. Animal tracks leave the trail whenever it takes a turn for the worse. I feel like doing the same but adhere to the beaten path, hoping that it will straighten out eventually. The weight on my back grows heavier with each passing moment. I keep going, though, telling myself that forward momentum must be maintained at all costs.

At dusk I curse the trailblazer as the trail climbs halfway up Mt. Carmel then levels out—one last meaningless ascent. I hobble down a side trail to David Logan Shelter in fading twilight. Sixteen miles and my feet are howling with pain. Never again will I blindly trust a map. Never again will I go so far in one day.

The shelter looks half-eaten. Porcupines craving salt have

chewed the edges of wooden bunks, the floor, the table—any surface touched by a sweaty backpacker. I hang my boots from one of the many nails protruding from the walls to prevent some porky from eating them while I'm sleeping. I hang as much gear as possible, including my pack with its salt-stained shoulder straps. I string a line across the front of the shelter for my hiking shorts, socks and t-shirts. My efforts seem futile somehow. Plastered with all my salt-ridden clothes and equipment, this shelter is now a porcupine's dream come true.

A thin ribbon of smoke coils through the thickening darkness from a yellow sparkle not far away. I spotted the campfire through the trees while making my way down to the shelter a half hour ago but was too tired to care. Now that I've dumped all my gear, I feel different about it. I sling a food bag, then go over to say hello. Surprisingly enough, my neighbor is a tall, slender woodswoman who came up the side trail this afternoon to spend a night alone here. She keeps the small fire smoking so that mosquitoes stay away. She looks quite comfortable sitting crosslegged before the fire. When I ask her if she'd mind a little company, she flashes a toothy smile that welcomes me. All the same, I squat down a respectful distance away.

We talk about wildflowers, peregrine falcons, bears and moose, then about the more mysterious aspects of the natural world. It's a refreshing change from the usual hiker's banter. I was ready to call it a night when I first landed in the shelter but conversation with this woodswoman rejuvenates me. Gulping down a liter of water and eating a half pound of gorp helps. Only when the fire dies away does it occur to me that I should excuse myself. It's getting late. I've imposed myself on my neighbor long enough. So I thank her for the pleasant chat, then limp back to the shelter to sleep.

In the morning, I am up and tending my fire before the woodswoman emerges from her tent. When she finally arises, she comes over for a brief visit. Then she breaks camp. All too soon she is on the trail and headed back to the lowlands. Loneliness nips at my heels while I drink a cup of coffee in silence. I hunger for more of the intimacy that I've just sampled but now it's just me and the chipmunks. Suddenly, I'm really missing my wife, Judy.

The worst thing about a campfire is how it slows down a hiker. But that's also the best thing about it. The hours slip away as water boils—one small pot after another. The campfire creates a window of calm in the swirl of daily activity. That's time enough to immerse oneself completely in the here/now, time enough for the surrounding forest to settle into one's bones. I listen to the creaking trees while tending the fire. I watch for creatures rustling through the leaves. Eventually, I build down the fire, adding smaller and smaller sticks to it until there's only a candlestick flame in a handful of twigs. When it diminishes to a pile of embers half-buried in grey ashes, I gather up my things. The fire dies with a one-quart dowsing. I let it smolder for a while, then douse it again. Soon enough, all my gear is wrapped up and ready to be packed. I soak the rocks encircling the campfire, releasing any lingering heat there. Then I stir water into the ashes until a cold, black muck is all that remains. When the rocks no longer steam, I pack up and go.

Back on the trail, I pick up the fresh tracks of a rather large herbivore. Definitely moose. I've been seeing moose tracks for a couple weeks but haven't actually spotted one yet. Moose range the entire length of the state nowadays but it hasn't always been this way. Only recently have they reclaimed all of Vermont's woods.

In 1853, Zadock Thompson wrote in his book, *The Natural History of Vermont:* "They are now exterminated from all portions of the state excepting the county of Essex, in the northeast part." And things pretty much stayed that way for more than a hundred years. But ten or twenty years ago, something caused their population to explode. According to wildlife biologists, there's been an influx of moose in the state since the early 70s. Perhaps a lack of predators precipitated the change. Or perhaps the gradual reforestation of Vermont did the trick—the state now being three-quarters wooded when it was once three-quarters cleared. Or perhaps disturbances in moose habitats elsewhere triggered a migration. Hard to say. But the fact remains: moose are almost as common in Vermont these days as they are in Maine. Moose are being spotted everywhere. They've been seen in Burlington, just outside Rutland, as far south as Manchester. Moose may someday be as numerous in Vermont as black bears or coyotes. The forest is chock full of possibilities.

At Bloodroot Gap I take a break, allowing the sweaty shirt sticking to my back to dry in a cool, western wind. I try to identify the lone songbird hiding in a nearby conifer. No luck. A brushy trail, obviously used by snowmobile enthusiasts in the winter, bisects the LT right where I'm sitting. I study the ever-changing sky. The clouds gathering directly overhead seem close enough to touch.

The rest of the day's hike is as effortless as that traverse past Chittenden Reservoir was supposed to be. The trail widens to a jeep track as it meanders downhill. I amble along, thinking that I could cover a lot of ground this afternoon. My feet disagree. They are still sore from yesterday, so it's probably for the best that I'm going only a bit farther. There's a footbridge across a feeder stream a half mile beyond the shelter just ahead. A couple hundred yards up that stream, my third food cache dangles over a small clearing in the woods. I'll make camp there and hang out for a day or two. Time for a rest. Besides, my clothes and equipment need a good cleaning, as does my body. It's getting to the point where my own smell is starting to bother me.

Three and a half weeks ago, I slung cache number three over a game trail. Hope the cord hasn't frayed. If everything inside the wooden box is okay, then I'm good to go all the way to Jonesville.

If not, well, then I'm headed for the nearest town. It's that simple. No big deal one way or the other, I suppose. Still, I can feel myself easing into an wilder frame of mind—slowly acquiring a natural perspective on things. Only twenty hours shy of the sixteen-day mark, it would be a shame to leave the woods now.

Thirteen

A RECENT WIND storm has dropped three large trees in the vicinity of my third food cache. The branches of the closest tree extend towards the dangling box. Another three feet and I'd be doing a salvage job right now. But, as the gods would have it, the box is unscathed. I lower it and check the contents. Everything inside is fine. Good. Now I have enough food to stay on the trail another week.

It's hard to say what is more surprising: how quickly vegetation has overtaken this place or how small the stream is—barely a trickle. What a difference three weeks makes! The small clearing where I had intended to set up camp is completely overgrown, so I string my tarp over a relatively open patch of earth between two old birches instead. I dig the leaf litter out of an old campfire circle, then tie back the spindly, protruding branches of striped maples. Gathering wood is ridiculously easy. The forest floor is covered with fallen branches. I have a large pile of kindling in no time. Before my sweaty t-shirt has a chance to dry in the slight breeze, I've carved a home for myself from the dense understory—only a minute or two from the trail yet far enough away to be out of sight. It's a quiet, sunny place in the woods. I call it Raven's Rest.

After dinner, I walk back down the trail to see if anyone has moved into Sunrise Shelter for the night. Sure enough, Husky and Mr. Clean are there, along with a petite, young woman. She is also hiking the Long Trail end-to-end. Her name is Wena or something like that. She is tending a couple blisters on her feet. I've had a great deal of experience with blisters over the years so I take a good look at hers. There are two bloody craters—one on each heel. They should have been patched twenty miles ago, when they were just hot spots of reddened, irritated skin. Not much can be done about them now. I don't say a word. Wena says her folks have a camp in Middlebury Gap, about twelve miles north of here. That's good. She can hole up there for a while, giving her feet a chance to heal on their own. Unfortunately, her trek to that camp is going be a long, painful one.

Like me, Wena is relying solely on purification tablets for drinking water but the water in her bottle doesn't have that tell-tale amber cast to it. I ask her why. She says the vitamin C tablets that she tosses into her water after purifying it neutralizes the iodine taste. The water also turns cloudy white, almost clear, in the process. I find this hard to believe but the expression on Wena's face convinces me that she's giving it to me straight. There just happens to be a small bottle of vitamin C tablets in the bottom of my pack. I tell her that I'll try it sometime.

Husky and Mr. Clean agree with me—that traverse around the Chittenden Reservoir was a miserable one. What kind of fool would cut a trail like that? We trade wild speculations about how the trail got that way, then I turn towards my camp hidden in the woods. Since I'll be resting up there a day or so, Husky and Mr. Clean will get far ahead of me. Probably won't see them again, so I wish them the best of luck while finishing the trail. They return the blessing.

I sleep well upon the soft, leaf-covered earth. Moose and deer skirt my camp during the night but it doesn't bother me. Since there's nothing particularly dangerous out here, there's no need to be afraid. One is safer in these woods than he or she could ever be in a city after dark. Sad but true fact.

First thing in the morning, I dig a large hole not far from the brook, then line it with a heavy plastic bag. In this makeshift sink, I wash all my dirty clothes. Afterward, I give myself a bird bath. These tasks take most of the morning since I have only a one-quart pot to draw water from the brook. But it's worth the effort. By noon there are clean clothes on a line strung across the clearing and my body is completely sweat-free for the first time in weeks. A hot sun quickly dries my clothes. I enjoy a lazy lunch while sorting my newly acquired supplies. And life is good.

Too many nuts! Now that I've tapped the third food cache, I have almost four pounds of them. What was I thinking when I packed for this trip? Seduced, no doubt, by the enticing calorie-per-pound ratio of this allegedly perfect food. But who could possibly eat so many nuts? I can't even stand to look at them.

While hefting a particularly large bag of nuts, I hear a loud crash down by the trail. Sounds like tools being dropped. I pull on my boots and race down to the trail, bag of nuts in hand. Through the brush, I spot three Forest Service employees digging waterbars and using a block and tackle to move huge, unwieldy stones. They look rather surprised when I step out of the woods, so I explain that I'm camped upstream. We chat about the moose in the area, about my hike so far, the weather, etc. Trail improvement is exhausting work. They wipe the sweat from their brows, welcoming a break in the action. But they aren't inclined to stand around talking for very long. When the crew leader says they'd better get back to it, I make my play. Poker-faced, I offer them the bag of peanuts. They accept the offering with beaming smiles. Hard labor requires incredible amounts of food. They set the bag of nuts aside and resume work. That's my queue to go. I slink back into the woods before they change their minds.

Years ago, trails were improved with wooden waterbars, corduroy and puncheon. Not so much any more. Untreated wood rots quickly, lasts ten years at best. Slippery, half-rotten wood can be hazardous. Unwary hikers often hurt themselves on it. Nowadays, most trail improvement is being done with stones. Stonework is much safer and holds up much better against the elements. But moving stones around is a lot of work.

Unlike the Green Mountain Club, the US Forest Service takes an aggressive, hands-on approach to trail maintenance—the more improvement the better. Consequently, the portions of the Long Trail that pass through the Green Mountain National Forest often get more attention than those that don't. Fact is, the Forest Service has more financial resources than the GMC could ever muster. The GMC employs a roving trail crew but can't match the Forest Service man-hour for man-hour. Volunteers from the twenty-odd sections of the GMC do what they can to help but volunteerism has obvious limitations. This is the major reason why some parts of the Long Trail seem so carefully manicured while others appear to be ignored. Trailwork requires a great deal of time, money and energy.

Back in camp, I lie about like a snake fresh from hibernation, sprawled across my foam pad with utter abandon. A brisk wind keeps the bugs down. When it fades away, I crawl under my netted tarp for protection. Between short naps, I study my guide book and maps, putting together a rigorous hiking itinerary. I hope to travel fifty miles during the next four and a half days, thus reaching Camels Hump by the Summer Solstice. That would put me in Jonesville the following day, June 22nd. For the first time since starting this long trek, I am seriously considering the possibility of going all the way to Canada. But the border is still a hundred and fifty miles distant and I have only two and a half weeks left. It'll be a push.

Aside from the big brag of it, there's no reason to hike the Long Trail all at once. Countless times I've told myself that it doesn't really matter how far I go. The main thing is to stay in these woods as long as possible. But there's no denying the powerful urge to go all the way. What difference could it possibly make? Why not stay right here in this delightful little camp until my food runs out? Stupid ambition, that's all it is. But as hard as I try to see through the mindless goal-obsession of it all, I still want to hike the entire trail. After all, I didn't sling food parcels across the state for nothing.

A strong wind kicks up at dusk, making it hard to burn the remaining pieces of the dismantled wooden box. I feed the flames one board at a time, keeping plenty of water on hand just in case. More than once, I tamp down the fire in order to keep it from licking the nearby brush. The surrounding forest is exceptionally dry. The wind is all bluster and attitude. Don't dare let down my guard until the last board is fully consumed and the fire settles down to a benign flicker. Afterwards, I douse the smoldering remnants.

The wind silences the downy woodpeckers that have kept me company all day. There must be a storm brewing. I search the patch of sky overhead for grey clouds but find only stars flickering in the dark void. Can't figure it out. I secure my camp against rain, just in case. Then I go to bed. The trees rock back and forth incessantly, creaking like old wooden boats moored in choppy water. At first I sleep fitfully, anxious about the impending storm, but the thick forest duff underneath me gradually unravels my nerves. And soon enough I am wandering aimlessly through a wilderness of dreams.

Fourteen

PREDAWN. WIND ROARS through treetops—a storm without rain. I'm out of bed and breaking camp with the first dim blue light. I eat a large bowl of raisin bran, then pack up. Raven's Rest disappears beneath the liberated branches of striped maples as I untie the lines holding them back. The empty campfire circle looks conspicuous, out of context. I start breaking it down but change my mind. Leave it for later. I'll be coming back here someday.

On the trail and moving fast. Recharged after a day off, I blast through Brandon Gap and up Mt. Horrid. The wind dies away. The anticipated downpour never materializes. I come upon a couple of overnight backpackers and ask for the latest weather forecast. They haven't a clue, so I assume that today will be another hot, dry one.

After Mt. Horrid, the trail eases over a succession of lesser summits along a high ridge: Cape Lookoff, an unnamed peak, Gillespie, then Romance. The Forest Service has chopped clearings in the woods at several places, creating scenic vistas. The Champlain Valley appears in the northwest, through an opening. Homecoming. Before the day's end, I'll be in the Breadloaf

Wilderness—an old stomping ground of mine. Excited by the prospect, I pick up my pace.

I stop for water at Sucker Brook Shelter and end up taking a nap. Awakening, I'm ready for the Mt. Worth climb. It couldn't be easier. On the other side of the mountain, the trail gradually winds down to Lake Pleiad. Dayhikers appear in groups of two and three—a sure sign that there's a big trailhead parking lot ahead. It's a sunny Saturday and the lake is less than a mile from Middlebury Gap. On the grassy ski slopes just before the lake, I come upon three middle-aged daytrippers lying about, soaking up the sun. We chat a bit. They are vaguely curious about my outfit, so I unzip my backpack to reveal its contents as a realtor might show a house. Then I ask if they'd mind running my mail into town. "Sure, why not?" one of them says. I hand over some letters, then excuse myself.

Something has changed. The forest has taken on a new attitude, or is it just me? All of a sudden, I have this intense desire to cover ground. My head buzzes with numbers: roughly 130 miles of trail behind me; 140 to go. I have 4 days to reach Camel's Hump in time for the Summer Solstice. Jonesville is 5 days, 50 miles away. I am carrying roughly 14 pounds of food. At 2 pounds per day, that's a 7-day supply. Numbers, calculations—suddenly long-distance hiking is all mathematics. Have I finally succumbed to the goal-obsession of it all? I've been on the trail 17 days already. Only 16 days left. Will have to cover a lot of ground fast in order to finish this trail in the time remaining. Making tracks today: 10 miles before lunch. Off to a good start.

Lake Pleiad is an alpine pond nestled in a pocket of woods between ski slopes. The place is all mine for the time being, so I strip off my clothes and go for a swim. Afterwards I lie naked on a patch of grass, drying under a hot midday sun, immersed in the elemental sensuality of it all. The subtle wildness of this place seeps through my flesh. The dark conifers skirting the tiny lake become my bones; the brackish water my blood. The lake's glassy surface is cratered by thousands of insects dancing silently in blinding light. My heart keeps time.

On a hunch that someone might show up soon, I slip back into my hiking shorts. Good thing. A young couple suddenly appears at the water's edge. Another pair arrives a few minutes later. Their overt displays of affection scratch the itch of my loneliness, so I shut my eyes and pretend I'm alone. Only fooling myself, granted, but it is better than longing for my absent wife. I consider getting up and leaving but the shelter where I intend to spend the night is only four miles away. No sense rushing there. So I open my eyes and gaze upward, ignoring the nearby couples. Billowy, white clouds drift past so slowly that they appear almost motionless.

A dragonfly lands on my leg. I shake it off without thinking. When it lands on my leg a second time, I try to remain still. The twitch comes anyway. A short while later, the dragonfly returns. This time I am a stone. The ancient, winged creature rests motionless on my knee for as long as it wants before flying away. It's a brief encounter, only a few breaths of divine communion. But that's long enough to acquire a different way of looking at things.

When the dragonfly darts away, I feel strangely calm, as if the primitive forces at work out here have just liberated me from all petty concerns. Suddenly, I am in a world as enduring as the elements themselves. I take a long hard look at the pond, gazing through the reflection of sky and self to see tiny lifeforms swimming around. The muddy bottom of the pond is as unfathomable as life itself. Its subtle wisdom eludes me but I become aware, at least, that there is more going on here than meets the eye. Only then does it occur to me that my journey into wildness is just beginning.

The climb out of Middlebury Gap is much harder than expected. I sweat like an iced glass in the oppressive afternoon heat, quickly gulping down most of the remaining liter of water. Big mistake not refilling my bottles back at the lake. Now I'm rationing water when I should be drinking as much of it as possible. Salt from dried sweat burns my skin as I struggle up Burnt Hill. I stumble along a ridgeline trail, searching the green chaos ahead for a glimpse of Boyce Shelter. When the shelter finally appears, a death-march smile rises to my cracked lips. There is a stream nearby, no doubt.

Down by the alleged stream, I am shocked to find only a few pools of standing water. A barely discernible trickle seeps into a bug-ridden sink between the rocks. I stir the pool into a muddy soup while anxiously dipping my water bottle into it. Not good. The dirt and leaf litter swirling about the pool take several minutes to settle down. During a second attempt, I'm more careful. It takes forever to fill one bottle. I repeat the procedure, drop a double dose of purification tablets into both bottles, then return to the shelter. It's a long half-hour wait before drinking. I pop a vitamin C tablet into one bottle just to see what happens. The result is amazing. Not only does the amber liquid clear with one good shake but it tastes like lemons. Thank you, Wena!

Dusk comes quickly. After cooking and eating a small package of ramen noodles, I string up my mosquito bar inside the shelter. Then I'm on my back, crunching numbers again while easing into dream country: 6 minor summits today; 14 miles traveled. 135 miles ahead of me; 135 miles behind. Exactly halfway now. The numbers, always the numbers. If dragonflies could speak, what would they say about these calculations of mine?

Fifteen

DAYBREAK. I AWAKEN to howling. It's a series of busy, high-pitched yapping sounds unlike anything I've heard recently. I force my eyes open as if to convince myself that the sounds are real. Still half asleep, I tell myself that it's just a bunch of dogs—three or four of them out there. Then I remember that I'm in the middle of the Breadloaf Wilderness. Entered it yesterday after climbing out of Middlebury Gap. Must be coyotes.

In the next moment, I hear the rustle and snap of a rather large animal breaking through the forest. Belly to the shelter floor, I catch a flash of brown fur down by the stream bed. A few moments later, a moose bounds into full view, slowly skirting the clearing in front of the shelter. When it's only thirty feet away, I search its eyes for some reaction. No alarm registers there, even though the moose has surely spotted me by now. How strange. It stomps through the brush unhurriedly. A calf appears in its leafy wake, anxious to catch up. I am inclined to shout something at it, just to be ornery, but remain respectfully silent. Life is hard enough for wild animals as things are.

By the time I'm fully awake, the moose are gone and the coyotes have stopped howling. Something stirs deep within me all the same. The surrounding forest is quiet and still. The wild hangs in the air like a lingering scent. It's good to be back in the Breadloaf Wilderness again.

In *Holy the Firm,* Annie Dillard wrote: "I came here to study hard things—rock mountain and salt sea—and to temper my spirit on their edges." While rambling through the Green Mountains, I graze the forest for whatever morsels of insight come my way. Forest ecology is a straightforward study; casual observations of animal behavior rarely illuminate; the linear trail underfoot offers few profound realizations. But every once in a while something happens, something appears out the corner of the eye, providing an opportunity to see through the mundane. It's nothing less than a glimpse of undiluted reality, a flash of the divine. At such times, I pay careful attention. I try to grasp the full significance of the encounter but that's extremely difficult to do. More often than not, the divine eludes me.

To study hard things—concepts as hard as granite. To study nature—that quasi-mystical relationship between all things animate and inanimate. To study concepts like God, humanity, the world and all those other vague, half-baked notions that surface whenever one is alone in deep woods. Two conscientious hikers might chatter emotionally about saving the earth as they pound a trail together but rarely do they dig deeper. In solitude, harder things emerge—things that resist definition; things that platitudes always miss; things that propagandists and advertisers cleverly avoid; the very things lost in translation whenever philosophy and religion become institutionalized, fossilized, hopelessly political.

Life itself, that ethereal subject, is the absolute hardest thing of all—a vexing cosmological ambiguity forged by the most mysterious forces of the universe. A great deal of effort is necessary to secure any truth concerning it. Such truths, buried deep in the earth, are as rare and as difficult to extract as diamonds. By contrast, half-truths are as easy to come by as acorns in autumn. In fact, it is nearly impossible to keep from stepping on them.

I cross two mountains, Boyce and Battell, before dropping down to Skyline Lodge to refill my water bottles. Then I cross three more: Breadloaf, Wilson and Roosevelt. I breeze through the Breadloaf Wilderness like a tourist doing a dozen countries in as many days. Information overload. My mind becomes a traffic jam of memories. How many times have I passed through these mountains? From every vista I see a valley where I've spent a small portion of my life—a few days camped over here, a couple days bushwhacking over there. I've walked most of the trails in these parts. I've fished every stream. I know this country as well as I know my own heart. Perhaps even better. After all, the heart changes steadily over time but this wilderness remains largely the same. The Breadloaf Wilderness is close to being the geographical center of Vermont—the wild core of a seemingly tame landscape. How could anyone spend much time in the Green Mountains without stumbling into this place? Every backwoods wanderer must wind up here eventually.

After panting over a rather insignificant summit, I brace myself for the seventh and last climb of the day: Mt. Cleveland. Low on water because I've been sweating so much, I lick my lips. I grunt all the way up the endless mountain. An easy climb under better circumstances, Mt. Cleveland feels like Mt. Everest this late in the day. The intense heat only makes matters worse. By the time I crest the summit, my skin is on fire—the salt-burn of dehydration stinging everywhere. I suck down a few last drops of water, then check my map to see how far it is to the cool, rippling stream hidden in Cooley Glen. Only half a mile and it's all downhill. Still, my parched lips lament the distance. Twenty minutes is a long time when the body aches with thirst.

Cooley Glen Shelter is an old friend. I stayed here several years ago during a west-to-east traverse across the Breadloaf Wilderness in the springtime. Back then it was so damp here that I couldn't start a fire. Now it's so dry I wouldn't dare. Hmm... So much for the concept of unchanging wilderness... The stream looks different. The shelter does, too. Even the trees around the shelter look different: older, taller, with all kinds of new growth lurking in their shadows. But the boards of the shelter floor, aged by weather, convince me that it must be the same place.

A young woman is camped alone here. She's a "wilderness ranger" from the Student Conservation Association. Apparently starved for company, she greets me with a big smile and a dozen questions. Despite my fatigue, I enjoy conversing with her. We talk about the weather, flowers, moose, everything imaginable. We do a food swap on the shelter floor like two kids trading marbles. I get her extra package of crackers in exchange for my unopened jar of peanut butter. It's going to be a delightful evening together, I start thinking. Just then two muscular, shirtless fellows about my age arrive from the south in a sudden wave of loud, sweaty bravado.

Despite the heat, the Shirtless Wonders gather together a huge pile of wood. Then they start a fire. It'll keep the bugs away, they say. I try to explain why that's a bad idea but they aren't listening. The "wilderness ranger" says nothing. With terrible swiftness, there's a bonfire crackling in the fire pit. A small dead spruce dangles over the edge, burning like an oversized match. A steady wind blows embers towards the shelter. I can't help but wonder how many GMC shelters have been lost this way. As a precaution, I fill every available container with water. Then I await disaster. Fortunately, the fire never blows completely out of control. It flares wildly at first but the Shirtless Wonders can't find enough readily available fuel to sustain it. All the same, I don't breathe easy until the spruce burns into oblivion.

The "wilderness ranger" gravitates towards one of the Shirtless Wonders for reasons only youth can understand. I suspect that she's been camped out here too long, that she craves more than just a little attention. When the touching begins, under the guise of a back massage, I consider moving out of the shelter. But that seems rather puritanical of me, so I choose to ignore them instead.

The other Shirtless Wonder tends the dying fire. I maintain a tether of polite conversation with him. I ask all the standard questions: Where did you start? How far are you going? How many days do you have out here? He tells me that they are on a six-day march from Middlebury Gap to Mt. Mansfield. That's a formidable twelve miles per day over the roughest terrain in the state. A tough trek under the best conditions, I wonder how they're going to do it in the prevailing heat. He says hot weather doesn't faze them. They've done this kind of thing before. Hardcore hiking junkies, they like a physical challenge when they go into the woods. The more rigorous, the better.

Back in the 1920s, when the Long Trail was still new, a good number of speedhikers took to the woods. At first they were rare among the ramblers but soon there were all sorts of hikers "racing up and down the Trail, trying to outdo one another and get themselves in the news." As Jane and Will Curtis reported in their book, *Green Mountain Adventure, Vermont's Long Trail*, the trail received "a good deal of unsolicited publicity which the Club soon wished would just go away." Members of the GMC swiftly concluded that speedhikers, with their headline-grabbing feats of physical prowess, undermined the spirit in which the trail had been blazed. After all, the founders hadn't built a race track. They had created "a footpath in the wilderness," enabling people to temporarily escape the tensions of modern living and enjoy the natural wonders of the mountains. So the GMC resolved to quell the trend. No longer would the Club mention Long Trail firsts in any of its publications, nor would it keep any time records. Speedhikers would be tolerated but they would not be encouraged.

No one knows for certain just how fast the Long Trail has been hiked or by whom. Back in 1927, a fellow named Irving Appleby supposedly hiked the entire trail in less than fourteen days, beating his own previous record. Surely it has been done faster than that since then. Just recently, a long-distance runner tried to do it in less than a week. Someday the record will be measured in hours and minutes. Some damned fool will sprint north from the Vermont/Massachusetts border at the discharge of a starting pistol and will be met at the other end by an official with a stopwatch. And the news hounds will gather around our hero at the finish line. No doubt some reporter will tout the run as a good example of humankind's indomitable spirit. And everyone will be duly impressed.

If I had the time, I'd shoot for a different kind of record altogether. I would hike the Long Trail as slowly as possible—taking months, perhaps even years to do it. What a feat that would be! Forward movement as a mere by-product of simply being in the woods—the ultimate achievement! But those who never finished the hike would have me beat. And the record would be held forever by some Zen master expiring in a half-lotus position on the starting line.

Sixteen

OUT OF BED at first light; on the trail by six. Already the temperature has crept into the high 70s. It never really cooled out last night. A heat wave is in full swing now. Rumor has it that the mercury will climb into the 90s this afternoon. The rain I slogged through earlier this month never made it this far north, so a dry spell is underway as well. The high ridge directly ahead, a bony four-mile spine between Mt. Abraham and Mt. Ellen, is a dry-mouthed traverse during even the wettest years. Running enough water through my system is going to be quite the challenge today. Figure I'll do the better part of the day's hike this morning, before it gets too hot. Get on top of Mt. Abe before noon. From there it should be a relatively easy ramble to the next camp.

Ten minutes out of Cooley Glen Shelter, I spot a bull moose moving through the woods. I slip behind a small spruce for cover as it snorts up the mountain. Since it's going my way, I try to follow. No good. The moose sees me the second I step into the open. It stretches its legs then takes off, trotting up the mountain with the graceful ease one would expect from a much smaller animal.

How ironic. After so many failed attempts to stalk moose, I

see them entirely by accident twice in as many days. But that's how it goes out here. Wildlife encounters usually come as something of a surprise.

By the time I reach the top Mt. Grant, my t-shirt is completely soaked with sweat. No doubt about it, today is going to be a real scorcher. Perhaps I should stop short of Mt. Abe and sit out this heat wave at Battell Shelter. That would be the smart thing to do. But no, I'm on the move now, pushing all the way to Glen Ellen Lodge. Got a good start this morning. Hiking strong. As long as I keep myself well-hydrated, I should be fine.

Seven-thirty. Deer aren't accustomed to seeing hikers on the trail this early in the day. I spook a pair of them halfway down the northern slope of Mt. Grant, then startle another one as the trail levels out. White tails bob through a green understory blurred by humidity. Fur flashes in the angular rays of sunlight breaking through the forest canopy. Once again, animal encounters are as sudden and as fleeting as dreams.

When the trail empties onto an open, rocky precipice called Sunset Ledge, I drop my pack. Then I drink as much water as possible. A steady southwest wind partially dries the shirt on my back—a brown t-shirt stained olive by weeks of salt. I search the thick haze for the vague outline of Bristol Cliffs Wilderness a few miles away. The Shirtless Wonders suddenly appear, enjoying the limited view only a minute or two before continuing north. No time to waste. They're all cranked up and moving fast. I don't expect to see them again.

The descent into Lincoln Gap goes quickly. I sign into a trail register in the gap, declaring to the world that I've been here. Then begins the long struggle up Mt. Abe—two and a half miles. Following the example set by the Shirtless Wonders, I strip off my damp t-shirt and travel half naked for a while. How incredibly comfortable! Why haven't I done this before? Feels like the temperature just dropped ten degrees.

I reach Battell Shelter with remarkable ease. Mid-morning.

Only one more mile to the summit of Mt. Abe. I chug down a second liter, then fill both of my bottles. Yesterday, a dayhiker gave me directions to a little-known water source located down a side trail in Holt's Hollow. There's no guarantee that I'll find it. Could be a long, dry hike to Glen Ellen Lodge. So I drink while I can.

In 1914, several years after the GMC was created, Professor Will Monroe moved to Burlington to teach foreign languages at the University of Vermont. Before long, he was hiking into the mountains every chance he could. He quickly fell in love with the Green Mountains—with Camel's Hump in particular—so he joined the GMC. After making a hefty donation to the Club, Monroe was commissioned to improve an overgrown, poorly marked portion of the Long Trail on the south side of Camel's Hump. He did just that. Then he took matters into his own hands ... .

Dissatisfied with the low-elevation trail he found farther south, well beyond Camel's Hump, Monroe set to work on a "skyline trail" stretching all the way to Middlebury Gap. Not everyone liked the idea. Some GMC members thought that the low-elevation trail cut by the Forest Service was good enough, that the Club should remain focused upon its primary task. After all, the dream of a trail spanning the entire length of Vermont was still a long way from being realized. No sense going off on tangents. But Monroe's trail became a rallying point for those more aesthetically inclined. His supporters weren't happy with the stump-ridden path passing through heavily logged portions of the forest, well below the summits. To them, a ridge-running trail was more in keeping with the Club's intention to create "a high, scenic mountain pathway." So they campaigned for the alternate route and eventually got their way.

Known today as the Monroe's Skyline Trail, this forty-mile section of the Long Trail rides the crest of the Green Mountains. Many GMC members consider it the main event. Those who hike this particular section of trail enjoy one great view after another. There's one problem, though: water is scarce along its highest ridge—the one between Mt. Abe and Mt. Ellen. Late in the summer or during dry years, water is practically nonexistent there. Great views, it seems, exact a stiff toll.

Intense sunlight washes over Mt. Abe's rocky, exposed summit. The air seems unnaturally warm. Visibility is limited to a couple miles by the thickening haze. There's no reason to linger. I polish off yet another liter of water, pull on the damp t-shirt to protect my fair skin, then go.

In Holt's Hollow, a sign reads: water 300 feet. I follow the side trail winding down through dense spruce until it empties into a dry, rocky crease in the land. Following the parched stream bed farther downhill, I stumble upon a couple shallow puddles of standing water. I use the lid of my bottle to ladle a liter of it. Then I return to the main trail. With two full bottles again, I'm sure that I can make it to Glen Ellen Lodge despite the blast-furnace breeze blowing steadily over the high ridge.

I lose steam on Cutts Peak. Another liter of water revives me. Mt. Ellen, the last climb of the day, isn't as daunting as expected. I arrive on top of it with energy to spare. But the long, gradual descent to Glen Ellen Lodge takes forever. My back aches, my knees complain. It's difficult to concentrate on the rocky path beneath my feet. I slip once, then a second time. My walking stick saves me from a bad fall. My pack weighs a ton. I adjust its shoulder straps but the pain in my neck doesn't go away. Each step is torturous. By the time I'm hobbling down the side trail towards the lodge, my legs are spent.

At Glen Ellen Lodge, an older woman greets me. She is hiking the entire LT north-to-south in a series of overnight outings. She says there is a remaining puddle of water below the dry spring nearby. I lie down on the wooden bunk, telling her that I'll get to it later. Learning that I've just hiked thirteen miles, the older woman lectures me about heat exhaustion. She's right, of course, but I congratulate myself all the same. Well-positioned now, I can easily reach Camel's Hump by the Summer Solstice.

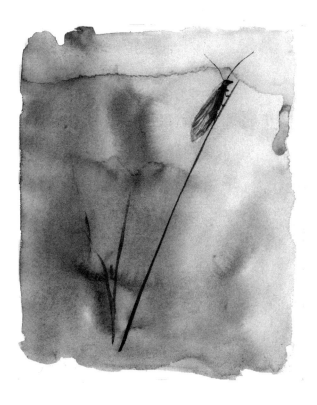

Seventeen

DESPITE EXCELLENT CROSS-VENTILATION, Glen Ellen Lodge holds the day's heat like a Dutch oven. Uneasy sleep in a feverish night. I rise slowly in the morning, feeling worse for having gone to bed. Lacking ambition, I putter about camp until mid-morning. Going only nine miles today. Good thing. I'm in no mood for another forced march in searing heat.

Slow creep along a ridgeline trail after ascending Stark Mountain, I walk a tightrope between two entirely different worlds. To my left is Buell's Gore, a triangle of unorganized woodland sandwiched between town boundaries. It's the southernmost tip of Camel's Hump State Forest. Wild country. To my right, a deforested slope drops towards a ski complex. Point, counterpoint. One would be hard-pressed to find a better example of Vermont's twofold nature.

As I gaze down the slope, I try to be fair. Skiers have as much right to these mountains as hikers do, I keep telling myself, but a wince comes automatically. Deep down inside, I know there's an unavoidable conflict of interests between those of us who want the Green Mountains to remain largely untouched and those who want them to be more user friendly.

No doubt the better part of the Vermont's wild uplands would become an unsightly sprawl of summer homes and resorts if it wasn't for Act 250—a statewide zoning law that went into effect a couple decades ago. I can pretend to be open-minded, arguing loudly in favor of landowner's rights, but I'm not oblivious to economic facts. Realtors and speculators are easily seduced by the profit potential of these mountains. Dollar signs can mystify even the most stubborn, old fashioned Vermonter. The wild can be subdivided and sold until there is nothing left of it. The ski slopes themselves play only a small role in the financial dream that twinkles in the land developer's eyes. That dream has many other parts: condos, shops, bars, hotels and restaurants. More often than not, development is a juggernaut.

What used to be a cottage industry is now big business. Interstate corporations vie for the thickest cuts of Vermont's recreation/tourism pie. Anyone who truly loves these quiet, thickly forested mountains can't help but recoil from the prospect of them becoming merely a playground for rich, out-of-state urbanites. Only Act 250 prevents that. Without it, the complete domestication of the Green Mountains would be a foregone conclusion.

The drop from Stark Mountain to Appalachian Gap is one of the steepest sections of trail in the entire state. I choose my footing carefully, grabbing exposed tree roots while negotiating a rocky trail stripped clean of its thin protective layer of soil. I pass a small group of fresh backpackers and warn them about the lack of water south from here to Lincoln Gap. They shrug off my warning with the casual indifference that I've come to expect. Chances are, they'll head home tomorrow afternoon with a touch of heat exhaustion—half-sick yet happy enough to have been outdoors for a short while. Only guys like me, on the trail for the long haul, are apt to give such matters any serious consideration.

In Ap Gap, I check the trail register to see how other end-to-enders are faring. Puff is a day ahead of me. Husky and Mr.

Clean the same. Uncle White, a guy I haven't met yet, has resumed his drive to Canada after a week away from the trail. I suspect that he's one of the three end-to-enders who hit the trail in May, a few days ahead of me. I'd like to meet the man but don't expect to catch up with him. It's apparent from the comments penciled in the trail register that he's moving fast.

The climb out of the Ap Gap isn't bad at all. I'm on top of a small mountain called Molly Stark in a half hour. On the other side of it, I stop at Molly Stark's Balcony to enjoy an excellent, fifty-mile view of the Champlain Valley. Camel's Hump is clearly visible to the north. Not so much heat or humidity today. No haze at all. Only an azure sky and sun blazing overhead. It's a great day to be in the woods.

The forest is under my fingernails. A mountain stream runs through me. My skin smells like the rotting leaves underfoot. I inhabit these woods no less than fleeting deer or chattering chipmunks. Three weeks on the trail and I belong in this green universe. The wind brushes over my face. I've given enough blood to the many biting insects to qualify as part of the grand design. My feet follow an unending path cutting through yellow lilies and bunchberry. My spirit soars high overhead, among the few wispy clouds. My heart sinks deep into the earth, as solid and unmoved there as the dark grey bedrock. My progress northward is deliberately slow, in celebration of the simple earthly pleasure of absolute immediacy. All heady presumptions have been stripped away by the wild. Today, this hour, this moment, I am a woodswalker. Nothing more, nothing less. And that once-and-future life of mine back in the lowlands is only a vague concept, a fading memory.

"The mountains are fountains of men as well as of rivers, glaciers, of fertile soil," John Muir once wrote. An unspeakable force flows from these rocky promontories, catching me off guard. I am re-created by it. This mere slipping between forest shadow and light is reason enough to be in the world. I inhale the freedom of the hills, exhale all paltry concerns. My walking stick has the airy strength of a prophets staff. Every pilgrim has his or her wilderness. This one is mine. I count my blessings as I walk—foremost among them just being in such a wonderful place. God is great. God is generous. The forest shouts timeless beauty. Here and now, it is impossible to be anything but fully alive.

Tall meadow rue is beginning to bloom along the trail—its tiny, white flowers bursting into starry constellations atop long, spindly stems. Wood sorrel hugs the ground—its candy-striped charm punctuating the leaf green cover. Canada mayflower laments the passing of spring—its fading petals dropping to the ground. Chickadees, ovenbirds and hermit thrushes delight in the riot of regeneration overtaking the forest. As I ease downslope towards Birch Glen Lodge, dark conifers fall away and the forest brightens with the broadleaf openness of birches, beeches and maples.

I take a midday meal at the lodge while basking in the warm light penetrating the canopy. Only two thousand feet above sea level, I am practically in the lowlands. But soon enough I'm moving upward again, climbing a long, stairless path that winds into the brushy Huntington Gap and beyond. Soon enough conifers mingle with birches and I'm back in that transition zone between northern hardwoods and the boreal forest. I flow with it, ever grateful for a chance to wander through this landscape's various moods.

In Huntington Gap, I spot a large patch of Indian cucumber root not far from the trail. Next thing I know, I'm on my hands and knees, fingering its delicious, white, carrot-like tubers to the surface. I squirrel away a dozen of them in plastic bag, then quit digging. No need to be greedy. A handful of tubers will make a nice snack.

I close the remaining distance between me and Cowles Cove Shelter, my resting place for the night. The trail narrows. The forest grows wilder. After crossing the biggest stream I've seen in days, I spot the shelter. It's a modest, forty-year-old structure perched atop a huge slab of rock. Nothing but trees in every direction. Only a few miles from the nearest road, this place is an unexpected find—a shelter in a pocket of wildness so close to the Champlain Valley that it seems implausible. I have stumbled into something rare.

Eighteen

THE FLORESCENT ORANGE embers of the dying fire glow in the darkness as I bed down. I fall asleep immediately. Next thing I know, the darkness is fading. Short night. Only a half dozen hours of sleep but, strangely enough, I feel well-rested. A quick breakfast and I'm on the trail before the morning sun clears the eastern ridge.

June 21st, the Summer Solstice. Big day. Three small peaks to surmount this morning, then Camel's Hump in the afternoon. I hope to rendezvous with my friend, Steve Bushey, before going over the Hump. I sent him a postcard a few days ago, asking him to meet me at Montclair Glen Lodge. After three weeks of hiking alone, I'm looking forward to some company. With any luck, I'll hook up with Steve around noon.

Another hot one. I peel off my t-shirt halfway up Burnt Rock. I've been feeling rather woodsy lately. Now I look the part: bandana, shorts and hike boots. My hair is dirty, disheveled and strawlike. I've taped a grouse feather to my walking stick. A pair of damp socks, a rotting bandana and a small towel dangle from my backpack. Despite the huge quantities of food eaten, I've lost a great deal of body fat. I've become a lean, green, hiking machine.

My pack is much lighter than it was when I left Raven's Rest. Having consumed most of my supplies since then, my entire outfit can't weigh more than forty-five pounds. Not light enough, though. I'll strip down to bare essentials at Jonesville. During the ninety-mile sprint from Jonesville to Canada, I won't carry anything extra.

The top of Burnt Rock has a distinctly alpine feeling to it, even though it reaches only 3,100 feet into the sky. A stony thumb protruding from stunted spruce, it has as much character as its taller neighbor, Camel's Hump, a few miles farther north. Ira and Ethan Allen Mountains rise from the intervening ridge with remarkable clarity in the early morning light. A cool breeze raises goose bumps on the surface of my skin. A sea of trees rolls away from my feet, sloping downward in every direction, towards the inhabited valleys not far away. I spot Burlington to the northwest. Strange seeing it there. Much like looking into the past. Before continuing north, I revel in a sudden outburst of exhilaration. I am jubilant, empowered, equal to any challenge. The sun promises a long day—the longest day of the year. I'm ready to go.

The Allens pose no problem at all. I attack them with inexhaustible gusto. I'm on top of Ira Allen in a flash and gazing northeast from a lookout on the other side of Ethan Allen's summit less than an hour later. Only the ragged descent to Montclair Glen Lodge gives me any trouble. My knees throb with pain as sharp as a toothache. My walking stick becomes a crutch, taking the full weight of my body and backpack as the trail drops away. I promise my knees a long rest soon but they don't stop complaining until the trail levels out.

At Montclair Glen Lodge, Steve and I greet each other with mutual surprise. Somehow neither one of us thought this rendezvous would actually take place. Steve pulls a big, juicy apple from his pack. He hands it to me, thus becoming my best friend in the world. Way too excited now, I pace back and forth chattering nervously while Steve tries to take a few pictures of me. An attractive, thirty-ish woman temporarily sojourned at the lodge with a heat-exhausted friend joins the festivities. She hands me a muffin. I chomp down on it hard, breaking away an already cracked tooth.

Steve is eager to take on the big rock directly ahead. High noon. Camel's Hump awaits. We fill our water bottles then charge up the mountain. Steve's long legs devour the trail with frightening ease. I move as fast as I can in his wake, gasping for breath between laughter and words. It's a hard pace to sustain but I'm driven by the sheer pleasure of Steve's companionship. I'd almost forgotten how good it feels to be with a friend.

Rising out of Wind Gap, I feel the impact of the previous three mountains. My pace slows considerably. Steve cuts his speed to match mine. He pumps me with questions, fueling my rambling monologue about the long trek from Massachusetts to here. Then he verifies a rumor that has been floating up and down the trail: the thermometers in Burlington registered 100 degrees Fahrenheit the day before yesterday. I was on that high ridge between Mt. Abe and Mt. Ellen at the time. Steve is surprised to learn that the heat didn't even slow me down. I've been drinking at least six liters of water every day. That's all I can say.

The sun beats down mercilessly as we rise above stunted spruce, wading through the crippled krummholz to bare rock. We sweat like fat, old men in a sauna. Even Steve is winded now. But the summit is in sight, so we pick up our feet to finish the ascent with one last burst of enthusiasm.

Steve is visibly disappointed by the view, dulled by afternoon haze. He's annoyed by the black flies swarming in the breathless air as well. I have grown accustomed to both. We share the summit with a dozen or more dayhikers, gathered on the exposed rock like a flock of seagulls on a denuded atoll. We make a hasty departure after slaking our thirsts. There's no reason to linger.

Steve tells me all about his labors in the lowlands as we drop down to a clearing just north of the summit. I have a difficult time relating to any of it. My life here in the mountains seems frivolous by comparison. All the same, I wouldn't trade places with him on a bet. At the clearing, we part ways. Steve takes a shortcut back to his car while I continue north along the LT. We shout goodbyes after each other from diverging trails, then ease into respective solitudes. A sudden pang of loneliness strikes while I'm hobbling down the trail. Good rendezvous—leave it at that. Will see plenty of Steve and all my other friends once I finish this trail.

During an extended break at Gorham Lodge, I talk with a GMC caretaker about water sources along the trail. Can't decide whether to keep going or stay here for the night. The caretaker is a nice enough guy and the screened lodge is inviting but there are four young backpackers on the trail right behind me. I suspect that they will turn this place into a party house this evening. So I keep going, onward to the Honey Hollow Tenting Area a little more than a mile away.

The descent into Honey Hollow is just steep enough to torment my knees. I am tired, the afternoon heat is oppressive and the bugs have found me. The last half mile is a study in backcountry misery. Arriving at the tenting area, a splash of cold water from the nearby stream changes everything. The steady murmur of the modest stream punctuates the delightful silence. The ambient forest couldn't be any more inviting.

A couple hours later, the backpacking foursome appears. They take over the two tenting platforms closest to the communal fire pit. I have strung my tarp in the woods thirty yards away, just in case they showed up. I greet the newcomers with a proprietary smile, pointing to the pile of wood I've dumped near the fire pit. "Help yourself," I say, then I finish my meager dinner of soup, crackers and hot chocolate. The young backpackers had wanted this tenting area all to themselves, no doubt, but they mask their disappointment well. They respond graciously to my welcome-wagon hospitality as they settle down for the night. And we get along just fine.

Nineteen

MY CAMP COMPANIONS call themselves The Fiddleheads. Two men and two women in their early twenties, they are a grunged-out, cafe-haunting crew smelling of patchouli. Earth children, free spirits, second generation hippies, they are out here to celebrate the Summer Solstice. They describe in detail the Grateful Dead concert in Highgate a few days ago. It was great, they say. The crowd swelled to 90,000. That's one dead-head for every seven Vermonters. Impressive numbers, indeed.

We sit around a campfire carefully tended by one of the women. We share a communal cup of herbal tea, trading stories as the cup slowly goes around. I keep it superficial for the most part, remaining aloof, recoiling from any overtures of true intimacy. I hope to link up with my wife in Jonesville tomorrow. Saving it all for her. I'll call Judy from the pay phone in front of the Jonesville General Store. With any luck, she'll be able to drop whatever she's doing and come meet me right away.

The Fiddleheads are quite considerate. They lower their voices after I go to bed, enabling me to doze off without difficulty. Well past midnight, I awaken to see their shadows still hunkered around firelight. They are still celebrating the Solstice. My thoughts are elsewhere. I sleep lightly on an empty stomach, dreaming of food.

In the morning, I'm packed and ready to go before any of my campmates are out of bed. The smoldering campfire looks like the epicenter of a blast. Food, clothes and gear have been strewn about the tenting area with utter abandon. I say goodbye to the young man watching me with a half-open eye. Then I slip silently into the forest. Breakfast on the trail is one last granola bar. Supplies are tapped now but I'll be in Jonesville in a matter of hours. Look forward to a big lunch there.

The walk through Honey Hollow couldn't be more pleasant. The trail empties into an overgrown logging road running parallel to a singing brook. Summer is in full bloom on either side of the trail: purple flowering raspberry, clover, cow vetch, hawkweed and daisies. The daisies remind me of Judy. Garter snakes slink away as I amble down the trail. My heavy footfalls flush them from the tall grass in the middle of the track. Robins perched high in shimmering poplars serenade the sun. The sky is the color of happiness. The temperature seems a perfect seventy-two degrees. I feel incredibly lucky to be here, strolling along an easy path on such a beautiful morning.

The forest opens to meadows as I approach a trailhead parking lot. A fellow about my age greets me with a broad smile. I stop to chat with him, leaning into my walking stick, offering my trail name before the stories begin. He, in turn, gives me his: Uncle White. Claims he was the first man on the trail this year. Two college kids started the same time he did but one of them got word of a summer job that couldn't be passed up, so they both quit the trail a week ago. That left Uncle White to spearhead this year's parade of end-to-enders. That is, until the heat dropped him. Uncle White says he fell flat on his face. Had to stop hiking for a few days but now he's thinking about getting back to it again. Uncle White says he likes to hike long and hard.

Says he doesn't want to bother with the LT if he can't do at least twenty miles a day. The prevailing heat makes such a pace nearly impossible to sustain. I shake my head, telling him that it has taken me twenty-two days just to get this far. Despite that relatively slow rate, I feel played out. Will have to rest up a day or two at a shelter on the other side of Jonesville before continuing north. Uncle White smiles broadly again, undaunted by my report. "I'll see you on the trail," he says with all the confidence in the world.

Jonesville seems like a bastion of civilization even though it's only a garage, a post office, a general store and a few houses. I haven't seen anything like it in a long time. The Long Trail passes right through it. At noon I enter the post office on a natural high, eager to pick up the parcels waiting for me. The postmaster is a well-kept, middle-aged woman who greets me with a fresh hello despite the fact that she sees backwoods tramps like me every day. She hands me a large parcel, then a smaller one, then a bundle of letters.

I ask the postmaster if she has seen any other end-to-enders lately. "Not today," she says. A pair of hikers came off the trail yesterday, though—a fuzzy-headed fellow sick with the heat and a tall thin guy with energy to spare. They were headed for Burlington, she says. That's Mr. Clean and Husky, I figure. The postmaster says the tall thin guy talked of continuing alone. Good chance that he returned to the trail this morning without stopping into the post office. When I ask if she has seen a guy with a white dog, the postmaster says no, she hasn't. Puff and Shed seem to have vanished. A week ago, Puff wrote in a shelter log that he was on his way to some rock concert. Maybe he never made it back to the trail. No telling where he is now—just a day or two behind me, or maybe elsewhere. According to the postmaster, about half of the end-to-enders never pick up their packages. Other thru-hikers get this far then quit. After all, it's 180 miles of rugged terrain from Massachusetts to here and another 90 from here to the Canadian border.

In front of the Jonesville General Store, I reorganize my things. I set a bag of chips and an open can of cold soda on the bench. There's an Italian sub in my belly now so I'm a happy camper. Inside the large cardboard box, I find a clean t-shirt and other much-needed supplies as well as food. The smaller box contains a stove maintenance kit and a tiny bottle of water purification tablets. Thank you, Judy! I've just purchased more food, ibuprofen and toilet paper from the general store. All set then. Can't think of anything else I need to pick up, so I sit back and read Judy's letters between repeated attempts to call her.

Stripping down. Everything nonessential must be jettisoned. Into the empty cardboard box goes fishing rod and tackle, binoculars, a filthy t-shirt, several empty fuel bottles, a bag of peanuts and whatever else I can shake loose. I heft the box. It weighs about five pounds. That's good but packing follows the purge. I stuff my backpack so full of food that my shoulders won't feel any difference for several days. That's okay. The payoff will come when it's most needed.

The noisy traffic jangles my nerves. Cars shoot past the general store like road-hugging rockets. After three weeks in the woods, I'm accustomed to much quieter sounds, to a much slower pace. A couple of potbellied fishermen stop and chat with me before going into the store. They can't figure out why my pack is so big. When I tell them that I'm hiking the length of Vermont, from Massachusetts to Canada, their eyes glaze over. It's a different world down here in the lowlands—a different world, indeed. I'm anxious to get back on the trail again. The sooner, the better.

Twenty

JUST AS I finish packing, my brother, Greg, casually walks up
and says: "Hey, how's it goin'?" He's dressed for a hike. Must
have heard the message I left on his answering machine an hour
ago. Says he received the postcard I sent from Middlebury Gap
and had been expecting my call. While I run back into the store
for one last junk food fix, Greg takes the five-pound box of
rejected gear and throws it into his truck. Then he offers me a
ride to the trailhead parking lot a couple hundred yards away. I
decline. I'm in no frame of mind for wheeled transport right
now, so Greg drives over by himself while I walk back. A few
minutes later, we head north together on the LT.

It's another hot day but Greg is all fired up for the short hike
to Duck Brook Shelter. He bounds ahead, full of energy. I slowly bring up the rear. He stops regularly, trying to adjust his springy
gait to my heavy-footed one. It's no use. Fully loaded again and
tired in a way that only a day's rest can fix, I grunt up the steep
trail rising out of Jonesville. No matter. We reach the shelter less
than forty minutes later. I break open my pack and commence my
end-of-day routine as soon as we land. Greg watches curiously.
Afterward, we scramble down to the roaring brook to cool off. I

strip off my shorts then slip into a deep pool. Greg only soaks his feet and wipes his neck with a wet bandana. Coming from the lowlands, he can't fully appreciate this bonanza.

We cover the picnic table next to the shelter with the assorted delicacies that we've hauled up the trail. We exchange news while eating. Greg talks about how hot it is in Burlington. I describe my life on the trail. The hours pass quickly. Greg lingers as long as he can but twilight is overtaking the forest already. I say nothing while he packs up his things. We part ways, agreeing to get together immediately after I finish this hike. Then Greg disappears into the foliage.

Once again, I'm surprised by the sting of sudden solitude. While getting ready for bed, I sink into a blue funk, brooding about the missed opportunity to connect with Judy. Wasn't able to reach her by phone. Tough break. I go to bed early to avoid the pang of loneliness that grows sharper in the darkness thickening around my campfire. Burlington is only fifteen miles away. I could go see her but no, I don't dare. If I leave the trail now, I won't finish. So I roll towards the shelter wall and go to sleep.

In the morning, I keep myself busy cleaning clothes, washing up and rebuilding my stove. One last day of rest before the big push to the border—make the best of it. It's a good day to lay low. By noon the forest is noticeably hot and humid despite ample shade. After a big lunch and a short nap, I begin to wonder why I'm so hellbent upon moving all the time. Why not just hang out here a while? Why not head into town and see Judy? Then I remember: Canada is still 90 miles away. I have only a week and a half left to get there. Either I finish this hike or give up the end-to-end ambition. There's no middle ground now.

Mid-afternoon, lounging about the shelter, deeply absorbed in my maps, I hardly notice the lean, sweaty hiker who suddenly appears. He makes himself at home in the shelter, taking over the lower bunk opposite mine. His name is Bruno. His eyes sparkle when he speaks. His thinning gray hair makes him look older than he is. He's a fifty-ish, French Canadian thru-hiker who left Massachusetts June 11th and hopes to reach Vermont's northern border in a week or so. He's a talkative fellow but admits that his English is "not so good." Our conversation is an awkward mix of Franglais, broken English and exaggerated gestures. All the same, I get the picture: Bruno is a long-distance hiker who lives for the sheer joy of intense physical exertion. Not your typical granola-munching athlete, he smokes two cigarettes and drinks a beer during the extended break. His lunch consists of a bologna sandwich and potato chips. He finishes it with a smacking of lips and a hedonistic grin. Then he cups his hands behind his head for a long afternoon nap. End-to-ender? A less likely candidate could hardly be imagined.

Looking at his lightweight, worn-out gear, I'd say Bruno has been burning up trails for a long, long time. But it doesn't make sense. How can such an athletic person have such non-athletic habits? Bruno offers no clue when he rises from his nap. He powders his feet and shoulders his pack before I can frame the question delicately. "Maybe see you later, ay?" he says with a generous, toothy smile. I nod my head in agreement, even though I don't expect to run into him again. Guys like me never catch up to guys like him.

Evening early. I carefully set the table, then eat my dinner in a civilized manner for a change. But this semblance of gentility only accentuates the difference between my current lifestyle and that more refined way of life in the lowlands. I long for cloth napkins, ceramic dishes, pleasant dinner conversation, maybe even a glass of red wine. Ten days, I figure, then I'll get back to it. Hot baths, fresh food, clean clothes—the thought of it all is too much to bear, so I force myself to think about something else. Tomorrow, the long ascent up Bolton Mountain. The day after that, I'll climb Mt. Mansfield. Should be able to reach my last food cache in four days. Clear shot to the border from there.

Twenty-One

THE TRAIL BETWEEN Duck Brook Shelter and Bolton Notch looks strangely familiar. Two years ago, I walked this stretch of the LT as part of a GMC trail clearing crew. A septuagenarian named Roland Boucher was the crew leader that day, supervising me and three other volunteers. Roland is dead now. I saw his obituary in the newspaper a month ago. All the same, I half expect to see him sauntering down the trail, holding a pair of hedge clippers like a dowsing rod and cutting away the protruding moosewood branches that most would ignore.

Roland's ghost doesn't materialize but I feel his presence here all the same. I come upon a patch of pale corydalis—late spring poppies still in bloom. A lover of wildflowers, Roland would have appreciated the way that their tiny pink petals are reflecting the early morning light. In one particularly large flower brightened by a sunbeam, I catch a fleeting glimpse of the old man smiling. No doubt about it, Roland still haunts these wooded hills, along with the ghosts of the many mountaineers that came before him. I can hear their shuffling footfalls in the distance—leaves crinkling and twigs snapping.

Passing the ten-foot-high stump of a huge old maple, I recall how it got that way. Using the chainsaw that I'd been hauling, Roland's friend, Herman, cut a downed tree blocking the trail so that the stump sprung back onto its roots. Clever trick. How many hikers passing this way notice the woody protrusion? It stands as yet another monument to those who have maintained this trail over the years. The trailside is littered with the bones of trees cleared away by dedicated men and women. I see them all around me.

There's nothing quite like hiking a stretch of trail that you've helped maintain. For the first time since I began this trek, I feel like a bona fide member of the GMC. Paying dues isn't enough. A little of one's sweat must go into the trail, as well. Approaching Bolton Notch, it becomes apparent to me how much more I need to do. This long hike only deepens my debt to those like Roland who have worked hard to keep the path open through the years. Without their efforts, the better part of the Long Trail would have disappeared into the brush by now. I feel a growing sense of responsibility. The torch is passing. Now that Roland and most of the old timers are gone, it's up to me and my generation to keep the dream alive.

The climb out of Bolton Notch is predictably arduous. I pace myself, moving as slowly as I can while still maintaining upward momentum. The trail levels out near Buchanan Shelter but the ascent is only beginning. Another hot day. I take a short detour down a cross country ski trail to a crease in the land where there is sure to be water. A few standing pools are hidden in the dense brush forty yards away from the trail. It will have to do. I eat as much trailmix as I can swallow between gulps of water, then continue up the LT. The dry timber all around me is mostly red spruce that has been decimated by the steady onslaught of acid rain over the years. Cracked earth and the withered leaves of false hellebore underscore the obvious. The ongoing dry spell is developing into a full-fledged drought. The rain that fell earlier this month wasn't nearly enough.

The Bolton ascent goes on forever. I am Sisyphus with a backpack, knowing that beyond this peak there are dozens more. The trail seems endless. No matter. This particular mountain can be my only concern right now. Such a brutal pitch! Not steep but groping uphill without pause. Finally reaching the top, I feel cheated. Bolton is one of the highest peaks in Vermont without a view. If the abandoned fire tower was operative, the story might be different. Unfortunately, the tower has been reduced to a mere suggestion of what it once was—no ladder or platform, just a skeleton frame. I take consolation in the fact that the toughest part of today's hike is behind me. It's mostly downhill from here to Taylor Lodge.

Halfway down Bolton's steep northern slope, I flop into Puffer Shelter for a short, much-needed rest. Then I hunt for water. The nearby stream bed is almost dry. I skim one last liter from a tiny puddle at the base of what was once a cascading waterfall. The shelter is a charming place with a nice view to the north. I'd be inclined to stay here if it wasn't for the lack of water. Probably for the best that I can't. Mine is a rather demanding itinerary. Have to make Taylor Lodge by the end of the day in order to stay on schedule. Racing towards the border now. No time to dally.

The trail beyond Puffer Shelter turns wild. It is narrow and overgrown in places, mostly roots and rocks. Few people travel this particular section of the LT. It's a bit out of the way. The dark, boreal forest closes around me as I reach the top of Mt. Mayo. The Clark/Mayo Col, a half mile farther north, is no less wild. In fact, the white trail blazes running through it are all that keep wilderness at bay. A few trees cut away on the eastern slope of Mt. Clark afford a nice view of Lake Mansfield a short while later, enabling me to orient myself visually. I enjoy the view for as long as I can tolerate the black flies, then finish the rocky descent to Nebraska Notch.

Approaching the notch, I pass a half-drained pond that looks more like a giant mud hole than a beaver's handiwork. There's a lone beaver swimming in tight circles in the middle of it. The poor creature seems disoriented, helpless. No doubt the beaver longs for rain even more than I do.

Taylor Lodge is another strangely familiar place. I've been here a dozen times. I used this lodge as a picnic site while working as a hiking guide a few years back. This time I share the lodge with a pair of backpackers, Anne and Sonny, who are hiking the LT in a succession of weekends. Seasoned backcountry travelers in their mid-forties, they've hiked extensively throughout the region. In fact, Anne and Sonny are members of that select group of hikers who have climbed every 3,000-foot mountain in New England. While I unpack, they regale me with stories of grueling ascents up mountains without trails. Having done my share of bushwhacking, I can almost feel the brush whipping across my face as they describe one particularly difficult climb. The trail-pounding that the three of us are doing these days seems easy by comparison.

The last of the dayhikers clear out of the woods at dusk. One pair stops by the lodge to chat before descending a blue-blazed trail to Lake Mansfield. I hand them a hermetically-sealed bag of trash with a sincere "thank you," then give Anne and Sonny my undivided attention. We talk nonstop, enjoying the camaraderie of long-distance hikers. But they surprise me by settling into their sleeping bags before the last bit of daylight fades away. Mt. Mansfield tomorrow, they remind me—Vermont's highest mountain. I putter about noisily a while longer, then follow their lead into slumberville. A brief downpour punctuates the quiet darkness around midnight but it isn't enough to excite any hope of replenished streams. In the morning when we crawl from our bags, there is no sign of the night's precipitation.

The southern approach to Mt. Mansfield, from Nebraska Notch to the Forehead, is the steepest section of the Long Trail. Rising out of the conifers, the ascent quickly becomes a rock scramble. A few wooden ladders have been fixed in place. Anne and Sonny left Taylor Lodge a half hour ahead of me but I catch up to them at the first ladder. Sonny is busy taking pictures of the cliffs looming before us, hoping to capture the essence of this dramatic landscape. Anne methodically picks her way through the rocks, carefully placing her feet, avoiding a sudden slip that could send her flying. I follow suit, then break ahead when the rock scramble reverts back to a walk-up ascent. Spectacular views make the climb seem easy.

The three of us rally at the Forehead, then travel together along Mansfield's high, rocky ridgeline. We hike past a busy tourist center at the end of a toll road. The Chin, at the top of the gradually sloping ridge, is the highest point on the mountain. Since it's Sunday, there's an endless procession of people walking up and down the trail from the tourist center to the Chin. They putter along like an army of ants at a picnic. An ambitious few have hiked up one of the rough trails that start at the base of the mountain but they stand out in the crowd. Most have just stumbled out of their cars after a long, winding ride up the toll road. Most sport tennis shoes and casual wear.

The Chin is abuzz with activity. Rocks have been carefully placed by GMC trail crews to better define the edge of the trail. It's an attempt to channel traffic through the fragile arctic/alpine vegetation near the summit and thereby lessen the impact. Not everyone complies. Some people scamper every which way over the rocks, seemingly unaware of the damage they are doing to the decades-old vegetation underfoot. The ranger/naturalist stationed atop Mt. Mansfield is busy trying to keep everyone off the remnant vegetation. His job is to educate the horde on the spot. Some people listen to him; some do not. All the same, the ranger/naturalist approaches the unthinking daytrippers with a delicate balance of tact and authority. His patience seems as endless as his concern for the fragile ecosystem. I marvel at such diligence. In their book, *Backwoods Ethics,* Laura and Guy Waterman listed ten places in New England that they consider "the backwoods equivalent of tourist traps." The Long Trail made the list. While I don't entirely agree with that assessment, there's no denying that certain summits in the Green Mountains get way too much foot traffic. Camel's Hump and Mt. Mansfield are especially hard hit. The latter is the most highly used alpine area in the state, thanks to the toll road. Over forty thousand people wander along Mansfield's high ridgeline every year. That's a lot of traffic for an area which consists of stunted spruce, sedge grass, mountain sandwort, wren's egg cranberry and various other flora that can be killed by a few careless footsteps.

In an attempt to divert a portion of the foot traffic to lesser-known places in Vermont, the GMC publishes *The Day Hiker's Guide to Vermont.* The book gives away many of the state's better kept secrets. It's hard to say how much pressure this publication takes off Mansfield, Camel's Hump or Vermont's other major summits—some, not enough. Meanwhile, the on-the-spot education process continues. But even the best efforts of the ranger/naturalists perched on top of these summits cannot stop the damage being done to the fragile arctic/alpine flora. Eventually, Vermont's few tundralike ecosystems will be destroyed. Either that or they will have to be cordoned off completely from the public. Fact is, some people just don't pay any attention.

"Loving it to death," the saying goes. Too much intrusion, no matter how well-intended, can only diminish the wild. The day is fast approaching when one will need a permit in order to visit a place like Mansfield's summit. And those permits will be hard to come by. With increased access, improved trails and roads, there might be no wild-ness left at all someday. A hundred years from now, everything wild might be humanized, managed, regulated into oblivion simply because there are too damned many us. Six billion people and growing .... In a world where the human population goes unchecked, all wild things must ultimately go the way of the dinosaur. There isn't enough room on this planet for both pristine wilderness and unlimited growth. Some difficult choices will have to be made soon. Either we get serious about limiting our numbers or say farewell to the wild forever.

Intense pain shoots through my knees on the downslope of Mansfield. I pull a neoprene brace over one knee. Between that and my walking stick, the descent is tolerable. Anne and Sonny converse with me all the way down to the road so that I have something other than pain to think about. All the same, I am glad when the ground finally flattens out.

Anne and Sonny hand me a couple granola bars then say goodbye. Their car is parked next to the road, along with a dozen others. Sad to lose their company but I'm too distracted by the constant stream of passing cars to dwell upon it. I amble up the busy road to Smuggler's Notch. At least a hundred automobiles roll by me on the mile-long stretch of blistering pavement. More people pass me in an hour than I've encountered during three and a half weeks of hiking. It's a bit overwhelming. Such sweet relief it is to finally get back to the trail, moving away from the road and deeper into the cool forest.

A steady stream of dayhikers files down the trail from Sterling Pond to the road. Late afternoon and everyone is going home. I fight the current like a salmon swimming upstream, pushing towards the pond with all the energy I can muster. My bare chest is slick with sweat. My hiking shorts are soaked. I gulp down as much water as I can stand but am still running dry. The passing, relatively sweatless tourists smell of perfume and soap. They stare at me as if they've never seen a thru-hiker before. I reach Sterling Pond just as the last of them are clearing out.

After dropping my gear at Watson's Camp, I stumble down

the trail on the far side of the pond to a rocky spot that allows easy access. There I strip off my clothes and slip into the water. I float like a waterbug on the pond's surface, between the super-heated air and chilled water, with a lunatic grin and happy splashes. I giggle skyward, reveling in the absolute delight of cool, wet relief before swimming froglike back to shore. Only then do I notice the rumbling in the pit of my stomach. Such a primitive way to live—from one sensual experience to another. The trail has stripped me down to fundamentals. The wild flows through me like an electric current. I can't imagine any other way of being fully in the world, of being completely here/now.

Twenty-Two

I UNPACK MY things at Watson Camp, then turn and greet Sterling Pond's caretaker as he enters. His name is Jeff. He's a twenty-something, mild-mannered man who takes his job seriously. He just said goodbye to the last of the dayhikers, while doing a little routine trail maintenance. With those duties performed, he has retired for the evening. In addition to being a refuge for thru-hikers like myself, Watson Camp is Jeff's home for the summer. It's a screened cabin about twenty feet square that overlooks the pond. I go to the porch to scribble in my journal and listen to the natural quiet. Jeff appears in the doorway a few minutes later. He confides in me as if we've been friends for years.

Jeff is still rattled from a bad encounter with a dayhiker this afternoon. A Christian fundamentalist, hellbent upon validating his own beliefs, tormented the young caretaker with carefully-worded phrases and biblical quotations. Hard to say how it got started. Jeff is too preoccupied with his own angst to tell me what triggered the dayhiker's outburst. Jeff wishes that he could have better explained his own deep-seated beliefs concerning the wonder and mystery of nature. He wishes that he could have successfully challenged the fundamentalist's practiced rhetoric. Born and raised in the bible belt, I scoff at the notion. I assure him that any attempt to reason with such people is an exercise in futility.

"Eternity is now," I declare rather boldly. In the brief tirade that follows, I assure Jeff that salvation lies in our ability to revel in God's creation, that damnation begins with a numbness to the world, that anyone who argues religion in a place as beautiful as this is beyond hope. Jeff agrees halfheartedly. He still feels that he failed, somehow, as spokesman for the wild. My attempts to console him are dubious at best. So we drop the matter, letting the sun burning bright orange over the pond finish what words can only start.

While fixing dinner, I find out that Jeff's troubles aren't altogether metaphysical. He has a headache that won't go away. He thinks it might be the result of his recent attempt to give up caffeine. He didn't bother replenishing his coffee supply when it ran out earlier this week. I laugh heartily as I pull a stash of instant coffee from my food bag. "Caffeine addiction should never be taken lightly," I tell him with feigned authority, then I make him a cup of joe. Jeff's mood improves dramatically with a few sips of the precious black liquid. I split the remaining powder into two bags, keeping one for myself and giving Jeff the other. He's overwhelmed by the gesture. He offers me food, the use of his Coleman stove and various other supplies in return. I decline everything but the food. Then we converse deep into the night, until I am too tired to continue.

On the trail again, day twenty-six. Over 200 miles behind me; some 60-odd miles ahead. A thick morning mist burns away as I climb up Madonna Peak. The five-note lament of a white-throated sparrow is almost lost in the loud hiss of whispering conifers. The ski trails that weave in and out of the Long Trail make it difficult to stay on track. I lose my way more than once, end up using the white trail blazes painted on trees to navigate the labyrinth. Beyond Chilcoot Pass, it's a different story. At that point things turn wild. I follow the overgrown trail winding towards the top of Morse Mountain, returning to a more familiar element. The hike down the north slope of Morse is a cinch—all daydreams and whistled tunes.

As I approach Whiteface Shelter, I spot someone taking a break. A moment later, Bruno and I are staring at each other with mutual surprise. I greet him with a simple "hello" to break the awkward silence. After telling each other what we've been doing the past couple days, our reunion doesn't seem so improbable. Bruno is fresh from a brief sojourn at a campground just below Smuggler's Notch. I, on the other hand, have been hiking hard for a change.

Raring to go, now that my pack is noticeably lighter, I manage to keep pace with Bruno. We leapfrog up Whiteface Mountain. On the downslope, we hike in tandem. Moving fast towards Bear Hollow Shelter, we trade stories in pidgin English until a set of animal tracks demands our full attention. We follow them for a quarter mile. The paw prints pressed deeply into the mud near a stream crossing are unmistakable. They are bear tracks—not more than a day old. During the next half hour, Bruno and I find other signs of bear activity: claw marks on trees, rotten stumps torn open for grubs, scat. The brand new shelter just ahead, we conclude, has been appropriately named.

According to the mid-19th century naturalist, Zadock Thompson, the black bear was once so common in the Green Mountains "that our Legislature continues in force a law allowing a bounty of $5 each, for its destruction." Nowadays, according to Fish and Game officials, there are about three thousand of them in Vermont. That's a good number of bears, certainly, but not quite as many as there could be. Their population is held in check by the bow hunters and riflemen who go after them in the fall. Consequently, spotting one in Vermont woods is a somewhat rare event. I have seen them only a half dozen times during my backcountry travels. Usually, I see only their rear ends as they're running away. They know trouble when they smell it.

Man and bear don't mix well. They never have. Bears will rummage through garbage given half a chance, making a real nuisance of themselves. As a result, some rural folk treat them the same way they would treat any other backyard pest. That attitude, combined with the annual hunting season, makes bears a bit skittish around human beings. They stay away from us for the most part.

It is often suggested that we might be destroying something necessary for our own survival whenever we destroy a part of nature. In his book, *The Great Chain of Life,* Joseph Wood Krutch offers some insight into this somewhat misdirected belief. He points out that humankind's ongoing preoccupation with its own preservation is not enough to assure the preservation of the natural world. Very little of the wild is essential to our own physical survival—perhaps none of it at all. We can get by without this particular plant or that particular animal. But the wild can survive "only if man feels the necessity of sharing the earth with at least some of his fellow creatures to be a privilege rather than an irritation." At the heart of the matter lies our relationship with bears, mountain lions, wolves and other large predators whose benefit to us is practically nil. Can we find it within ourselves to coexist with such creatures or must we force them into free-range zoos? What if they cause trouble for us? Do we have a right to kill them?

After seeing a few bears up close and personal, I have developed a tremendous appreciation for them—not because they are especially majestic creatures and certainly not because they are gentle, warmhearted ones. Simply put, they represent an alternative way of life on this planet. And that, I believe, is reason enough for us to find a way to cohabitate with them. I do not fear bears, wolves or wildcats nearly as much as I fear living in a world that has been completely tamed. Then there will be no chance of us becoming anything more than the arrogant, self-absorbed, self-serving creatures that we are now. Only those relatively large, toothy creatures keep alive any hope of our eventual rehabilitation. Once they have all been either domesticated or eliminated, we will have no choice but to live in a world entirely of our own making.

Bear Hollow Shelter is a clean, well-built, relatively new structure that seems altogether modern compared to the past few camps. Bruno and I quit hiking early in the day. Tomorrow Bruno will go into the thriving metropolis of Johnson, Vermont for breakfast and more supplies, while I stay in the woods and tap one last food cache. This shelter seems an appropriate place to rest up before pressing farther north. The surrounding forest consists mostly of birches and maples so there's a good mix of light and shade here. A slight breeze, temps in the 70s, bugs not bad at all. The leafy quiet sets a pleasant tone. At first Bruno and I lounge about like a pair of hobos but that doesn't last. Before sunset, we break out maps and start poring over them. Mentally if not physically, we are still on the move.

Sunrise. Bruno leaves camp before I finish eating breakfast. An hour later, I am on the trail right behind him. The earthy path underfoot gradually transforms into a jeep track, then into a logging road as it gropes towards the Lamoille River Valley. A squadron of deer flies are circling. They take turns attacking the fleshy, exposed crown of my head. I snatch them from the air one at a time, longing all the while for a protective breeze. The breeze never comes but I manage to lose the flies, anyway—right before reaching my fourth and final food cache.

Opening the cache, I marvel at the fact that everything inside is just as I left it over a month ago. Since this particular container is made of plastic instead of a wood, I knew that it would hold up well to the elements. Still, it's a surprise to find it undisturbed. Hard to believe that neither man nor beast stumbled upon it. Since I'll have to retrieve this container after finishing my trek, I leave an extra bag of nuts in it, along with an empty fuel bottle and some dirty clothes. It takes only a minute or two to seal up the container and sling it back into the trees. Then I return to the trail.

It's an easy walk down to Route 15. I follow the highway until it crosses the Lamoille River. A quick jog westward on a county road, then I'm back on the white-blazed trail and easing into the woods. I take a break at a rocky promontory called Prospect Rock, basking in the sun. I fall in love with Vermont all over again, while admiring the pastoral scene in the valley below. Then Bruno appears out of nowhere. He hands me a fresh brownie from a bakery in town. He asks me how far I'm going today. Corliss Camp, I say. He says he'll meet me there, then he disappears into the trees.

Late afternoon, after surmounting three low ridges, I encounter a couple of old friends, Jan and Sue, at the base of Laraway Mountain. Like me, they are ex-guides hiking the LT for the sheer joy of being outdoors. We chat a while, then separate abruptly. Time is tight. They move southward, headed for a gap a hundred miles away. I keep moving north.

I hyperventilate up Laraway Mountain, feeling the day's long journey in my leg muscles. The descent to Corliss Camp is especially hard on the joints. I limp into the camp then drop my pack. Bruno looks up from maps sprawled over the picnic table and says, rather nonchalantly, that he hadn't expected me for another hour. Then he congratulates me for covering fifteen miles of rugged terrain in one day. I'm a bit angry at myself for having hiked so far. I boil up water for dinner then go to bed early. It takes two ibuprofen to dull the aches and pains enough so that I can fall asleep.

Twenty-Three

DAYBREAK. ONCE AGAIN, Bruno leaves camp just as I am starting breakfast. I shout goodbye after him, suggesting that we might see each other again in a couple days. Then I finish a cup of coffee in deep woods solitude. In the full light of day, Corliss Camp is a depressing sight. Most of its glass windows are covered with plastic. Some damned fool intentionally broke them out. It boggles the mind. GMC camps are open to anyone who wants to use them. To destroy such places is akin to shooting oneself in the foot. But no, other people suffer as well. Vandalism is a sinister pleasure. I give the camp a much-needed sweeping since that's all I can do to improve it, then hit the trail.

The Butternut climb is easy in the cool, early morning mist. I ride the contours around Basin Brook, softly humming tunes. My songs can't compete with those of the wood thrush, though. Its melodic, flutelike notes ring from every corner of the brightening woods. As I stop by a feeder stream, a male thrush lands on a nearby branch. It sings boldly, as if its life depends upon making music. Suddenly the tedium of my endless groping north disappears as I realize just how lucky I am to be in such a wild place, observing such a beautiful singer.

It always happens this way. Just when I'm on the verge of losing interest, just when the green infinity seems uniform and uninspiring, something comes along to shake me out of my indifference. A female thrush answers the male's call. She is fast approaching, from tree to tree. In the next minute, the two thrushes come together and it's a marvelous thing to behold. They flutter about each other in a dance older than the forest itself. As long as thrushes inhabit these mountains, as long as their songs ring through the trees with incredible clarity, I will believe in the wonder and glory of creation. Such joy these simple creatures generate! How impoverished our lives would be without them. God is generous, indeed, filling the world with winged musicians.

Bowen Mountain is also an easy ascent but the long, brushy ridge between its north and south summits is a study in misery: mounting heat, menacing deer flies and a gauntlet of stinging nettles that set my exposed calves and thighs on fire. I am glad to be done with it, descending the ridge a half hour later to a jumble of rocks called Devil's Gulch. My legs wobble as I hop from boulder to boulder. Too many days of hard hiking. I trudge into Ritterbush Camp in the early afternoon, then call it quits. Only seven miles covered today but I don't dare go any farther.

Ritterbush Camp is no palace but it suits my needs. I just want to lie down. Any broad, flat surface will do. I break open one of the half-dozen paperbacks leaning against the wall on a cobwebbed shelf in the camp. It's a pulp fiction mystery of the worst kind yet I thoroughly enjoy reading it. Afterwards, I sprawl across a wooden bunk with absolute abandon, dreaming of better books. That's one more craving to fulfill upon returning to the lowlands.

At dusk, four rowdy teenage boys and a dog roll into camp with partytime written all over their faces. Typically loud and boisterous on the trail, they settle down considerably the moment they spot me standing in the doorway. I've been listening to their approach for ten minutes, so I've had plenty of time to consolidate my mess and make room for them. But they don't take up residence inside the camp. They pitch tents behind it, instead. Apparently, they're in no mood to get drunk or high in front of an old fart like me. No matter. They are quiet as they go about their festivities and that's more than I could have hoped for. I go to bed early, nodding off long before sundown. In the morning I return the favor, scratching about camp like a mouse, packing up my things as quietly as possible. Only the dog notices my departure.

Mid-morning in the fire tower atop Belvidere Mountain, I sit cross-legged on a platform between flights of stairs while assessing the situation. June 29th. I've been on the trail almost a month now. I feel somewhat refreshed after an extended rest at Ritterbush Camp but my joints still ache. Am thinking I should wrap them before continuing any farther north. But I don't do it. Instead I ignore the pain and enjoy the view. To the south is Mt. Mansfield and the Sterling Range—already a good distance away. Looking the other direction, there's Jay Peak—not far north at all. The Canadian border is just beyond. A few more days and I'll be there. Hardly seems possible.

At Tillotson Camp, I consider opening a can of soup resting on a shelf. I decide against it. Someone might need it someday. I'm not that hungry. I've been consuming incredible quantities of food lately. Don't know what's wrong with me. Seems like my belly is always growling, even though my supplies are disappearing faster than expected. Go figure. I drink an entire liter of water before leaving Tillotson, then refill my bottle from a nearby trickle. Keep myself hydrated—that's the main thing. Sweating and drinking, sweating and drinking... It's an endless process. My body is a bucket full of holes.

Beyond Tillotson, the trail is narrower and wilder than it's been in a long time. I get the impression that only thru-hikers like me ever travel this way, that everyone else has forsaken this part of the LT. There are fallen trees all over the place, as if some childish god had thrown a temper tantrum here recently. I bushwhack around the blowdown whenever it's too thick to climb over. Progress is slow. The heat intensifies as the sun rises higher, monopolizing the sky. It's been a while since I last saw a dark cloud—a couple weeks, anyhow. Could really go for a good storm right now. Even thunder and lightening would be welcome. But no, the land will remain parched today. The sky is too blue. Might as well be hiking in Southern California.

In the saddle between Tillotson Peak and Haystack Mountain, the forest gives way to a relatively new beaver pond. My boots sink into the muddy trail around it, frightening some frogs and salamanders. The thinned trees beyond the pond are a chaos of living and dead conifers that limit visibility to twenty yards. Here the forest is dank—the pungent smell of fungus mingling with rotting spruce, fir, moss and fern. But a patch of white flowers rises triumphantly from the decay. They bloom in loose clusters atop long stems. Wild orchids, I suppose. Hard to say for certain. I've never seen anything quite like them before. How odd. Just when I thought I knew all of Vermont's wildflowers, a brand new one pops up—as precious as a clear morning sunrise in high summer.

It's a long, steep descent from Haystack Mountain into Hazen's Notch. My knees aren't happy at all. Every step is painful. I carefully avoid rocks and roots, leaning into my walking stick as much as possible. When the trail finally levels out, I breathe easier. But I am limping by the time I reach the dirt road cutting through the notch.

In Hazen's Notch, I take a long break before doing the last mile to the next camp. I flag down a passing automobile and hand off the last of my postcards. Strangely enough, the older couple in the car takes my mail without giving the matter a second thought. One of the postcards is especially important, urging Judy to come get me in three days. If she receives the postcard in time, I won't have to wait for her in North Troy more than a few hours. The departing car shoots down the road in a cloud of dust. I plant my walking stick in the dry earth, then struggle to my feet.

A twenty-minute walk gets me to Hazen's Notch Camp. Bruno is standing in the doorway like he owns the place. He claps his hands together as I hobble down the trail. Says he has been expecting me for hours. I tell him that I'm feeling pretty beat up. Bruno smiles broadly, offering me one of the two beers that have been chilling in the brook. Then he produces the pound of fresh hamburger purchased in Montgomery this morning. He gives me half. I can hardly believe it. I've been daydreaming about fresh food for days, about hamburger in particular. I must have mentioned it to him back at Corliss Camp. He says he thought it would be a nice surprise.

We immediately fire up our stoves and fry the hamburger along with some onions that Bruno also brought from town. I break out my dwindling supply of instant coffee. Afterwards, Bruno and I glow with bellyful contentment as we trade speculations about water sources along the last section of trail ahead. Daylight diminishes ever so slowly. We putter about camp as long as we can, then surrender to the inevitable. We slip into our sleeping bags and are down for the count before darkness overtakes the camp.

Twenty-Four

BRUNO IS UP and moving about camp in the middle of the night, stirred to action by bad dreams. He packs up his things, telling me that he is making for the border today. I wish him the best. I suggest that he take the abandoned plastic bottle on the stove, fill it with water and carry it with him since water is supposed to be scarce on the other side of Jay Peak. Bruno insists that he doesn't need it. He tightens the miner's light strapped to his forehead, then departs with a curt goodbye. His footsteps fade into the rhythmic sounds of the torpid night. I go back to sleep, happy enough to rise with the sun later on.

By 7 a.m., I'm on the trail and following Bruno's tracks over the shoulder of Sugarloaf Mountain. Already the air is thick with heat and humidity—a recurring theme these days. I cut my pace on the other side of the shoulder but it's too late. My hiking shorts are soaked with sweat already.

One last parade of small summits: Bruce, Buchanan, Domey's Dome and Gilpin. Up and down a brushy ridgeline trail barely visible in places, I mindlessly follow the white blazes like a cow going to the barn for milking. A large pile of scat convinces me that there's a bear in the neighborhood. I tread softly for a short while, excited by the prospect of seeing it. Then I come to my senses. The chance of a full-grown bear showing itself in the bright light of day is practically nil. Besides, the scat wasn't that fresh.

Toads leap from the trail, a ruffed grouse explodes from the undergrowth, ravens soar overhead. I have all the familiar creatures of the forest to keep me company today. A huge garter snake coils into a fighting stance after I prod it with my walking stick. I apologize for being so rude, then move on. The forest extends in all directions—same old story. I grow a bit weary of this infinite green world yet shudder at the prospect of actually leaving it. For the first time in a month, it occurs to me that I'll be doing just that very soon. I am tired of this constant movement, tired of being hungry, sweaty and sore but am not quite ready for that easier life back in the lowlands. I need a few more days.

Early afternoon. I reach Jay Camp after a steady, five-hour march along the LT. Lately I've been alternating short hiking days with long ones to make the knees last. So far the arrangement has been working. Today's a short one. Tomorrow I'll do a twelve-mile push to the border. My plan isn't as ambitious as Bruno's but it'll get me there. I open the camp, read the shelter log and clean up my things. Then it's time to relax. Regular rest, I have come to believe, is the better part of endurance.

Clouds gather right before dusk. Is it possible? I pull all my gear into the camp just in case. Miraculously, the overhead sky darkens. In the next moment, fat raindrops crater the dusty earth. I tilt my head upward while standing in the camp's doorway, letting a few drops hit my face. I close the door only when the rain starts beating loudly against the roof. The deluge doesn't last. One good soak then it's over. The flame of the candle planted on the camp table flickers in the cool breeze stealing through the open window. I lie on top of my sleeping bag, mesmerized by the sound of drizzle pricking the darkness. Then my mind slips out of gear. I force myself awake just long enough to blow out the candle.

Morning ascent up Jay Peak through a thick, airless fog. The shrouded conifers haunt the mountainside like phantoms from a more primordial era. I ignore the slight chill in the air as I mount the rocky trail. My mind turns with weighty matters now, as if the time has come to reap a harvest of natural insights. I ponder the complex relationships between God, nature and humanity as I ease uphill. It's a rare wandering/pondering frame of mind— one that perfectly suits the mountain's mood this morning. My head is only a vessel collecting its simple declarations.

God is that which creates order out of chaos—the ultimate paradox of the universe. Nature is the sum total of all that is ordered and unordered, known and unknown. The very essence of our humanity is tied inextricably to wild nature, yet it is precisely the wild that suffers most from our thoughtlessness and hubris. How terribly ironic! We congratulate ourselves for all the technological advances we've made over the millennia, as if our problems could be solved by mere technique alone. How quickly we forget natural history. When we reach the end of our evolutionary tether, it's doubtful that we will perish in a blaze of apocalyptic self-annihilation. More likely, we will fade in a whimper of bloodless detachment. Perhaps the civilization we have been building will outlast nature as we know it. To what end? As the wild goes, so goes our collective soul. Love and care—it all comes down to that. What matters most? Either we love the world or we hate it. There is no middle ground. In the final analysis, either we revel in creation or we disparage it. The choice is clear.

Atop Jay Peak, I sit on a benchmark embedded in the rock. As my thoughts settle down, the thick fog enveloping the summit breaks apart, exposing valleys both immediate and distant. Lake Champlain comes into view—a thin blue gleam of light just below the western horizon. Clouds prowling the Green Mountains scatter before the rising sun. A chilling wind cuts through me. I am pleasantly surprised by it, urged back to my feet and compelled to move. A nearby building emerges from the fog, reminding me that this is a busy ski area during the winter. I quickly traverse a grassy slope then dart back into the woods as if escaping civilization, even though there's no one on the mountain right now but me.

The Long Trail tumbles downhill, then winds towards a wilder summit, North Jay, where only thru-hikers like myself ever go. The ferns hanging over the trail give me a thorough soaking as I wade through them. At first I resent their chilly caresses but it's such a refreshing break from the usual sweaty dampness that I can't help but enjoy it. Running cool now, I could go on like this forever. Unfortunately, the border isn't that far away.

During the 1920s, the Long Trail crept farther north, bit by bit, until it stretched all the way from Massachusetts to Jay Peak. In less than two decades, the GMC had cut a trail through most of the state, almost reaching the Canadian Border. Quite the feat. But in 1929, Roy O. Buchanan, a UVM professor renown for his accomplishments as leader of a work crew called the Long Trail Patrol, decided to change that. With his brother Bruce, he bushwhacked north for three days, from Jay Peak to International Boundary Marker 592, selecting a route for the final leg of the LT. "We were tired of that "almost"," he said later on. Two other club members, P. D. Carleton and C. G. Doll, came through the following summer to actually cut the trail. Then it was complete: a footpath spanning the entire length of Vermont.

No big deal, some would say. What's the Long Trail compared to the Appalachian Trail or one of those remarkable conservation measures undertaken out west? No world-class feat, granted, but the fact remains: twenty years after a schoolmaster gazed into the

Green Mountains, the dream of America's first long-distance trail became a reality. We who live in Vermont and press our tracks into this trail on a regular basis have every reason to be grateful for the hard work done by those who came before us. There is more at stake here than mere recreation. This "footpath in the wilderness" has given us full access to a wilder part of the landscape, to a Vermont rarely mentioned in tourist brochures. The Long Trail is as much a part of our lives as the rugged mountains themselves. Our debt to the trailblazers runs high.

At Shooting Star Shelter, I refill a water bottle from a seep in the nearby ravine as a mounting breeze suggests the possibility of rain. The sky overhead is featureless. Returning to the trail, I can hardly believe what my senses are telling me. The sky is growing darker. The air is cool, wet and restless. Then it strikes, just as I am climbing up Burnt Mountain—a sudden downpour drenching me to the skin in minutes, transforming the trail into a stream. I revel in it, slipping a hat over my head but otherwise forsaking raingear. I welcome the cool embrace of a summer afternoon cloudburst. All smiles and laughter, I cross one last road before the rain lets up, invoking a stare from a passing motorist. A better ending to the long dry spell could hardly be imagined.

The hike up Carleton is an odd mixture of sweat, drizzle and chilling breeze. Out of necessity, I put on my rain jacket to finish the day's hike in relative warmth. A pair of southbound thru-hikers, as fresh as wild lilies in early spring, stop me for a brief trailside chat. I recite a litany of nearly dry water sources between here and Mt. Mansfield before realizing that this afternoon's deluge has probably changed all that. My spellbound audience ignores the rain-soaked forest surrounding us as they listen to me. Surely they see the dust in my eyes. Or perhaps they are mesmerized by the filthy, dripping wet, wild-eyed ragamuffin standing before them—a vision of themselves a month from now. With weather-beaten skin, bandaged joints and strawlike hair, I must be quite the sight to behold.

Using my walking stick to propel myself at top speed along the muddy trail, I thoroughly enjoy the flattening terrain, not giving much thought to what it implies. Despite the dozen miles I've put behind me today, I've gained a second wind. But suddenly I'm looking at a sign announcing the end of the Long Trail. The white blazes that I've been following for weeks disappear. Beyond the sign, a few yards down the trail, there's an absurd-looking monument encircled by brush: International Boundary Marker 592. And it's over, just like that. Now I can only follow the blue-blazed trail pointing eastward, running parallel to the Canadian border, descending slowly to Journey's End Camp.

I wander down the side trail in a swirl of disbelief. My legs find their way to the camp by themselves. The earthy, barely discernible trace underfoot has seen little traffic lately. The daylight playing through the open hardwood forest illuminates the wet, bright green verdure on the forest floor. An absolute calm fills the air.

When I reach the camp, I go through my regular routine as if tomorrow will be just another day on the trail. Not until I read Husky's, then Bruno's, triumphant entries in the shelter log does the full weight of the moment strike home: I have finished hiking the Long Trail. My time in the woods has come to an end.

Twenty-Five

SUNDAY, JULY 2ND. I take my time breaking camp since there's no reason to hurry. Down by the brook, the mist hanging over a small waterfall holds me captive long after I finish splashing water on my face. The hawkweed and daisies scattered through the tall grass in front of the camp require careful inspection. Breakfast consists of coffee with a little hot chocolate mixed into it. I drink it down slowly while staring into a cold fire pit. Then I pack up and go. Hunger is the prime motivation now. A few nuts, some tea bags and a little powdered milk are all that remain of my food supply. But North Troy is only four and a half miles away. There will be a general store in that village, no doubt. Should have a full belly before noon.

In less than an hour, the trail becomes an overgrown jeep track, then a logging road, then a graded town road. The forest gradually fades away. The town road intersects a two-lane gravel road. The land flattens to broad pastures dappled with high-summer bloom. A passing automobile dusts me every once in a while, otherwise I have the gravel road all to myself. Crows replace ravens. Robins sing loudly. The gravel underfoot becomes pavement. Over a slight rise, the road empties into the sprawling village of North Troy. I walk past barking dogs tethered to huge maples shading manicured lawns. Motorists ignore me. End-to-enders must be a common sight in these parts.

Sitting on the sidewalk in front of the general store, I wolf down glazed donuts between gulps of fruit juice. Then I tightly clutch my water bottle like a derelict hugging his only comfort. A steady stream of locals passes in and out of the store. It's Fourth of July weekend and everyone is stocking up on beer, ice, charcoal and other holiday supplies. An old man arranges chairs around a podium on a flatbed trailer parked across the street. Folk music blares over loud speakers. A sudden gust of wind knocks the American flag off the trailer. I limp over and pick it up. The old man tells me that a parade will pass this way in a couple hours. I'm looking forward to it.

A strangely familiar car pulls up to the curb. Not until Judy pops out of it do I begin to grasp what is happening. "You're so thin," she says as she kisses me hello. I give her a big hug, then throw my backpack into the trunk. The passenger's seat of the car feels obscenely luxurious. I sink into it, still clutching my water bottle. Judy puts the car into motion and away we go. The Green Mountains dart past, one wooded summit after another. We cruise towards Burlington with terrible swiftness. I grope for bearings, wondering how long it'll take the calluses on the bottom of my feet to soften up, how much body fat I'll regain, how many days will slip away before I can get back into the woods. Then I stare out the side window at the passing landscape.

"No amount of word-making will ever make a single soul know these mountains," John Muir once wrote of his beloved Sierras. After hiking the LT, I understand what he meant by that. I now have a knowledge of the Green Mountains that can only be acquired through the flesh—a sense of them that runs deeper than mere utterances, images or ideas. More importantly, I know my place in this incredible world. These mountains are my home. And that, far more than the brag of peak-bagging or long-distance hiking, is what I've gained.

The forest is under my fingernails. A mountain stream runs through me. I am no less wild than a bear or a moose. Things that were important to me a month ago no longer matter. I am free—as free as any creature can be within the brackets of mortality. And it's a very good feeling. But I know from experience that this feeling can't last. All too soon, the simple reality of the wild will be obscured by the complex abstractions of a much more domesticated lifestyle. In due time, I'll start forgetting what I am. Then I'll have to drop whatever I'm doing and head for the hills for yet another reminder.

ABOUT THE AUTHOR

Walt McLaughlin has backpacked extensively throughout the Northeast during the past twenty-five years. Since receiving a degree in philosophy from Ohio University, he has worked as a bookseller, hiking guide, outfitter and freelance writer.

His poetry and prose have appeared in *Adirondac, Appalachian Trailway News, Vermont Life* and many other periodicals. Also in print is a narrative of his brief sojourn in the Alaskan wild, *Arguing with the Wind,* along with a collection of essays entitled, *Stalking the Sacred.*

Walt lives in St. Albans, Vermont, where he is the director of Wood Thrush Books. Visit him at www.woodthrushbooks.com to browse his unique selection of nature poetry and prose titles. To request a catalog or contact Walt, email him at wtbooks@sover.net, or write to:

Walt McLaughlin
85 Aldis Street
St Albans, VT 05478

A Death on the Barrens by George Grinnell

Five young men canoe through Canada's arctic and must find their way home, after the death of their leader, Art Moffat, from hypothermia. Winter closes in, the group runs out of food. The book is both an account of a journey through then unmapped northern lakes and rivers, and a story of the spiritual awakening of the young men on the trip. A Death on the Barrens was first published in 1996, and quickly sold out. This second edition contains watercolors by Roderick MacIver. 182 pages.

#6075   A Death on the Barrens – $19.95

True North by Elliott Merrick
with an introduction by Lawrence Millman

In 1929, at the age of 24, Elliott Merrick left his position as an advertising executive in New Jersey and headed up to Labrador to work as an unpaid volunteer for the Grenfell Mission. In 1933 he wrote True North about his experiences in the northern wilderness, living and working with trappers, Indians and with the nurse he met and married in a remote community. The book describes the hard work and severe conditions, along with the joy and friendship he and his wife experienced. 320 pages

#6078   True North – $19.95

Sleeping Island A Journey to the Edge of the Barrens by P.G. Downes

In Sleeping Island, Prentice G. Downes records a journey made in 1939 of a North that was soon to be no more, a landscape and a people barely touched by the white man. His respect for the Native Indians and the Inuit and their ways of life, and his love of their land, shine through this richly descriptive work. With the kind permission of the Downes family, Heron Dance has republished this book. 288 pages.

#6056: Sleeping Island – $19.95

A Natural Wisdom—Gleanings from the Journals of Henry David Thoreau

Walt McLaughlin selects 80 thought-provoking and insightful entries from Thoreau's journals. 60 pages.

#6019   A Natural Wisdom – $10.00

The Laws of Nature—Excerpts from the Writings of Ralph Waldo Emerson

Another inspiring collection edited by Walt McLaughlin. 35 pages.

#6018   The Laws of Nature – $7.95

Earth, My Likeness—The Nature Poems of Walt Whitman

A carefully selected collection of poems alongside Rod MacIver's watercolor art creates a grand tribute. Edited by Howard Nelson. 144 pages.

#6071   Earth, My Likeness – $11.95

This Ecstasy by John Squadra

This courageous and beautiful book of poems explores, with simplicity, the truths of love and a spiritual life. Some poems are very erotic. Some poems expose the truths of life we all share.

#6043   This Ecstasy – $10.95

Heron Dance Book of Love & Gratitude

Heron Dance celebrates the open heart and the beauty and mystery that surround us with this book of poetry, book and interview excerpts. 48 watercolors by Rod MacIver and selections from the written works of Helen Keller, Dostoevsky, and Henry Miller, among many others. 80 pages.

#1602   Heron Dance Book of Love & Gratitude – $12.95

HERON DANCE

Heron Dance is a nonprofit 501(c)3 organization founded in 1995 by artist Roderick MacIver and run today with his wife Ann O'Shaughnessy. It is a work of love, an effort to produce something that is thought-provoking and beautiful. Through our website, quarterly journal, workshops, free weekly e-newsletter and watercolors, *Heron Dance* celebrates the seeker's journey and the beauty and mystery of the natural world.

We invite you to visit us at www.herondance.org to view the many nature watercolors by Roderick MacIver and to browse the hundreds of pages of book excerpts, poetry, essays and interviews of authors and artists. In our gallery store, we offer *Heron Dance* notecards, Limited Edition prints, and originals as well as dozens of hard-to-find books, music and films.

To receive our free weekly e-newsletter—*A Pause for Beauty*—which features a new watercolor and a poem or excerpt, just click on the *Pause for Beauty* link found on our website or contact us at the number below.

www.herondance.org • 888-304-3766
heron@herondance.org

NOTES FROM THE TRAIL...